William Bacon Stevens

The Sabbaths of our Lord

William Bacon Stevens

The Sabbaths of our Lord

ISBN/EAN: 9783743325036

Manufactured in Europe, USA, Canada, Australia, Japa

Cover: Foto ©ninafisch / pixelio.de

Manufactured and distributed by brebook publishing software (www.brebook.com)

William Bacon Stevens

The Sabbaths of our Lord

THE

SABBATHS OF OUR LORD

BY THE
RT. REV. WILLIAM BACON STEVENS, D.D., LL.D.
BISHOP OF THE DIOCESE OF PENNSYLVANIA.

PHILADELPHIA
J. M. STODDART & CO.
733 SANSOM STREET
1873

Entered according to Act of Congress, in the year 1872, by
WILLIAM BACON STEVENS,
In the office of the Librarian of Congress, at Washington.

WESTCOTT & THOMSON,
Stereotypers and Electrotypers, Philada.

HENRY B. ASHMEAD,
Printer, Philada.

CONTENTS.

	PAGE
PREFACE	11
INTRODUCTION	17

CHAPTER I.
The First Sabbath at Nazareth 39

CHAPTER II.
The First Sabbath at Nazareth (*Continued*) 54

CHAPTER III.
The First Sabbath at Nazareth (*Continued*) 65

CHAPTER IV.
The First Sabbath in Capernaum 82

CHAPTER V.
The First Sabbath in Capernaum (*Continued*) 100

CHAPTER VI.

The First Sabbath in Capernaum (*Continued*) 117

CHAPTER VII.

The Sabbath at the Pool of Bethesda 134

CHAPTER VIII.

The Sabbath in the Corn-Fields 159

CHAPTER IX.

The Healing the Withered Hand on the Sabbath 182

CHAPTER X.

The Second Sabbath in Nazareth 199

CHAPTER XI.

The Healing of the Blind Man on the Sabbath 218

CHAPTER XII.

The Healing of the Blind Man on the Sabbath (*Continued*) 238

CHAPTER XIII.

The Healing of the Woman who had a Spirit of Infirmity, on the Sabbath 257

CHAPTER XIV.

Dining with One of the Chief Pharisees on the Sabbath ... 275

CHAPTER XV.
THE SABBATH AT BETHANY.. 294

CHAPTER XVI.
OUR LORD'S SABBATH IN THE SEPULCHRE................................ 313

CHAPTER XVII.
THE FIRST LORD'S DAY. I.—THE MORNING HOURS.................. 331

CHAPTER XVIII.
THE FIRST LORD'S DAY. II.—THE EVENING HOURS................. 347

CHAPTER XIX.
THE CHANGE OF DAY FROM THE SEVENTH TO THE FIRST............ 366

PREFACE.

THE following work has two designs. First, to give an expository account of our Lord's words, and works on the Jewish Sabbath, while he tabernacled in the flesh. By grouping together the sketches of his Sabbaths, as recorded by the several Evangelists, and separating them from other material, we bring into clearer light, and undistracted observation, the sayings and the doings of the Lord of the Sabbath, and thus learn more clearly what is his mind and will, in reference to the divine command, "Remember the Sabbath day to keep it holy."

Secondly, to make a small contribution to the literature of the Sabbath question.

This question has a wide compass, and a full discussion of all the points involved in it would fill volumes. Hundreds of books, more or less elaborate, written by the most thoughtful and educated men, have been published on all the branches of this important subject, so that it is doubtful if there is any one phase of it which has not already been fully discussed. The controversies of past generations, however, are being revived in this. The discussions which at different times, raged with such fierceness around the fourth commandment, are reappearing now, though in new forms and dress, corresponding to the modern aspects of thought and action.

So important a place does a Sabbath, or holy rest-day, hold in every Christian country, and in the Christian Church, that its sacred observance will ever call out the bitter opposition of the prince of darkness and his human allies. It needs but a slight knowledge of the "signs of the times" to see what inroads are already being made in desecrating the Lord's day, and what efforts are put forth to weaken the tone of the public conscience on this point, and to make us relax our hold upon it as a divine and obligatory institution.

We cannot be blind to the fact, that in various parts of this land, open attempts are now made to turn this rest-day into a continental Sunday, and make it the weekly gala-day of society through all its grades. We shall soon be called upon to meet these questions face to face. They rise up in our literature, in politics, in social life, and we cannot shrink from them. The keeping holy of the Lord's day, is essential to the very existence and perpetuity of our nation, and it becomes all Christian men, and especially all ministers of Christ, to stand upon their watch-towers and give the needed note of warning as the danger of wresting it from us approaches, that the people may take heed to the incoming evil and learn the true nature, the real value, and the divine sanction, of this holy day. For it is a day essential to the well-being of the individual, the family, the Church, the nation and the world; to the best interests of man in this life, and to the higher interests of his soul in the life which is to come.

These biblical sketches of "The Sabbaths of our Lord" may perchance throw new light into some minds on these important matters. They may also serve a profitable purpose for family reading on the Lord's day. They can be used perhaps with wider interest by the many lay-readers in the Church, who may find in these pages instruction, guidance and pleasure. They might be useful to Sunday-school teachers, and furnish a whole winter's course of instruction to many Bible classes. Thus they may be the humble means of fixing in the minds of the young and the old, the fundamental principles which underlie the Lord's day, and on which we base its origin, its obligation, its perpetuity and its unspeakable blessings.

The late John Quincy Adams, President of the United States, in closing an address before the delegates of the National Lord's Day Convention, used the following significant words:

"It was the remark of one of the ablest and purest of those foreigners who came to our aid in the days of revolutionary peril, and who made his home, and recently his grave, among us—the late venerable Peter Duponceau of Philadelphia—that of all we claimed as characteristic, our observance of the Sabbath is the only one truly national and American, and for this cause, if for no other, he trusted it would never loose its hold on our affections and patriotism. It was a noble thought, and may well mingle with higher and nobler motives to stimulate our efforts and encourage our hopes. And while it is the glory, so eagerly coveted by other nations, that they may be pre-eminent in conquests and extended rule, let us gladly accept it as our distinction, and wear it as the fairest of all that grace our escutcheon, that we pre-eminently honor the Sabbath, and the Sabbath's Lord."

W. B. S.

PHILADELPHIA, November, 1872.

"Sundays observe; think when the bells do chime
   'Tis angels' music, therefore come not late:
      God then deals blessings. . . . .
Let vain or busy thoughts there have no part,
   Bring not thy plough, thy plot, thy pleasures thither;
Christ purged his temple, so must thou thy heart.

GEORGE HERBERT.

JERUSALEM.

INTRODUCTION.

THE OLD-TESTAMENT SABBATH.

WE have in the four Gospels the record of quite a number of our Lord's Sabbaths. They show us where he was, what he said, and what he did, on this day of rest. They bring before us a great variety of facts, places, scenes, and a series of holy teachings uttered by our Lord in various cities and villages of Judea. We shall thus be hearing from week to week the words of Him who "spake as never man spake," the holiest of preachers, on the holiest of days.

It is interesting to know how He "who made all things," and who, as the Creator of heaven and of earth, "rested on the seventh day from all his work which he had made," and who, in consequence, "blessed the seventh day and hallowed it," would do when he came to the earth which he had made, to save the men whom he had created.

It is interesting to see how He, who gave Moses the law of the Sabbath, would act under his own law when he tabernacled in the flesh.

It is interesting to mark how "the Lord of the Sabbath" would conduct himself in reference to those many and onerous glosses and traditions, with which the Scribes and Pharisees had encumbered the fourth commandment, whether he would tacitly acknowledge their authority or sweep them away, by his word and example, as so many human incrustations on the divine law.

These points will be illustrated as we proceed, and we shall gain new and interesting facts concerning our Saviour's personal history by attentively studying the records of his Sabbaths after his public entrance upon his ministry as detailed by the several Evangelists.

Before we enter upon these separate Sabbath sketches, let us turn back to the old Hebrew Sabbath, and look at its origin, history and design. As to its origin, it was instituted at the end of the six days' work of creation by God himself, and was designed to commemorate his rest on the seventh day "from all his work which he had made." Hence "he blessed the Sabbath day and sanctified it."

By "blessing the Sabbath day" we are to understand that he designed it to be fountain and source of blessing, for only thus can time, which has no personality or consciousness, be blessed. He therefore constituted this day as one fraught with special blessings.

By "sanctifying" the seventh day we understand, in accordance with the use of Old-Testament language, the hallowing or setting it apart from other days by specific acts and consecrating it for an holy purpose.

Thus on the first page of Revelation we find these three great facts, that God, having completed the works of creation, "rested the seventh day from all his work that he had made"— that a seventh day's rest, or Sabbath, was in consequence thereof designated for all the future as a day of blessing, or a "blessed" day— that this seventh portion of time was henceforth, by divine ordering, to be set apart as "sanctified" time, and kept apart from all secular uses and pursuits.

These are the trinal roots of that great institution which, ordained by God himself and exampled forth to us in his own holy rest from creative work, was by him specially charged with blessing, and by him specially separated and sanctified for his service and man's welfare.

The name *Sabbath* given to this day comes from the Hebrew *Shábath*, which signifies to rest, whence *Shabbáth*, the day of rest. The root of these words is *Shéba*, or seven, a number which, not in the Hebrew tongue alone, but in the language of most of the Eastern nations, signifies fullness, completeness or perfection. Hence we find in those nations, as the biblical and classical scholar well knows, septenary divisions of time, consisting of cycles of seven days, or seven months, or seven years, which can be accounted for only by referring them back to the seventh-day rest after creation, the traditions of which spread themselves over, and rooted themselves in, the languages of the Eastern nations.

These things link the Sabbath with God as its author, with the finished work, creation, as its first day of observance, and with man as the being to whom pertains the blessings of this sanctified season. It thus has a divine basis, a worldly basis, a human basis, and is as universal in its obligation as the world in which it was first proclaimed, and is as enduring in its perpetuity as the human race, for whose special blessing and sanctification it was ordained. While in the succeeding patriarchal times we find no formal mention of the Sabbath, yet we notice numerous indications of it appearing here and there, showing with conclusive force that the institution was still preserved, though in the lapse of centuries and in the wide dispersion of the human race its obligations were less heeded and its observance less marked and regarded.

Over two thousand years pass away before we again meet with any formal notice of this day. The time and the occasion of its reappearance were both interesting. The children of Israel, to the number of nearly three millions, and under the leadership of Moses, had escaped from Egypt, had crossed the Red Sea, had gone a month's march on their way to the promised land, and were now encamped in the wilderness between Elim, with its wells and its palm trees, and Sinai, so soon to smoke at the presence of God. The people had murmured for water and for bread. God gave them manna from heaven. Of this bread the people gathered an "omer" (six pints) for each person, except that on the sixth day they gathered "two omers for each person." This Moses explained by saying, "This is that which the Lord hath said, To-morrow is the rest of the holy Sabbath unto the Lord." "Eat that to-day, for to-day is a Sabbath unto the Lord; to-day ye shall not find it in the field; six days shall ye gather it, but on the seventh day, which is the Sabbath, in it there shall be none." This transaction took place one month before the delivery of the Law on Mount Sinai, and therefore was but the resuscitation or the bringing forward again into prominent view the old organic law of God in Paradise.

Again, therefore, did God determine to re-institute his almost forgotten Sabbath, and to re-enact it under such circumstances as should strike the beholder with awe and illustrate his own majesty. Hence, on the top of Sinai, upon which he had descended in fire, and up to which he had called Moses, and amidst thunderings and lightnings and earthquakes, he gave the ten commandments and wrote them with his own finger upon two tables of stone, as if too jealous of their sacredness and their accuracy to permit Moses, or even Gabriel, to be an amanuensis on so solemn an occasion. Remarkable indeed must those laws be, which God did not trust Moses, his great prophet—no, nor yet angels or archangels—to write out or even copy from his mouth, but which he must write with his own finger, and on tables, not of brass or gold of man's make, but of stone of his own handiwork, that man might have the exact and literal transcript of his will, so that there should be no possibility of mistake as to its words or its meaning. The code of laws, or ten commandments, which God thus gave on Mount Sinai is the moral law of the world, given at that time in special charge to the Jews, because to them were to be committed the oracles of God, and deposited by Moses, at God's command, in the ark of the covenant; the only laws thus secured, but designed, by their very tenor, for the whole world, and recognized as such by our Lord and his apostles, and by the Church of God wherever found.

The law of the Sabbath stands as the fourth

of these commands. It is graven on the same stone tables with the other nine; it was written with the same finger which wrote the others; it was deposited under the mercy-seat in the ark of the covenant, and between the outstretched wings of the cherubim in the holy of holies with the rest; and if the other nine are moral laws, the fourth is also; if the fourth is not, the other nine are not. If the nine are designed for all men, so is the fourth; if the fourth is not designed for all, neither are the other nine. They stand or fall together. The attempt made by men who would relax the obligation of the Sabbath to sever the fourth command from the Decalogue, and designate it as ceremonial and partial, is a rude dislocation of that command from its true articulations and attachments that destroys at once the majesty and symmetry of that moral code, the ten laws of which seem to be the ten fingers of the two hands of God, whereby he upholds the moral government of the world.

The majesty of this fourth commandment comes out more clearly if we dwell a moment on its peculiar construction. It was ushered in by an emphatic word which marked no other—

"Remember!" not only implying that they should recall the original institution of their patriarchal Sabbath, which tradition, perhaps, had handed down; but also implying that they should give this command in special charge to their memory, that it might not be forgotten throughout all their generations.

It is drawn up with a minuteness of specification which we find in no other command. It is based, as none other is, on God's special example. It is the only one linked with his special blessing and hallowing. It is the only one given both negatively and positively. No command was more frequently repeated, none more carefully guarded; and it is the only command of which God said that it was a "sign" between him and the children of Israel, throughout their generations, for a perpetual covenant, and this peculiar language is repeated no less than four times by Moses and Ezekiel.

To those, then, who calmly look at these points, it becomes perfectly clear that the fourth commandment is of perpetual moral obligation, —that it is still binding with all its original force, —that it demands of us the same obedience which we pay to the first, the sixth or the tenth, for it is as much the expression of God's will, and as much the requirement of God's authority, as any one in the Decalogue.

It is to be observed, in this connection, that there are two phases under which the law of the ten commandments is to be viewed: 1. As a code designed for the whole world; 2. As a code specially adapted to the Jews; and these two phases are discernible in the very structure of the Decalogue, as a moment's contemplation will show.

The germ, the root-principle, of each of the ten commandments is invariably enunciated as a distinct proposition, and in the briefest and most emphatic language; *e. g.*, the second commandment, which in our Bibles is divided into three verses, is all expressed in the original by three or four words—Thou shalt not make to thyself idols. The third commandment in four words—Thou shalt not take up the name of the Lord thy God in vanity. The fourth commandment in five words—Remember the rest-day, to hallow it. The fifth in four or five words—Honor thy father and thy mother. The sixth, the seventh, the eighth, the ninth, in two words each, and the tenth, though occupying several lines, is really contained in the two Hebrew words translated Thou shalt not covet. So that the entire ten commandments are comprised in the original Hebrew in less than forty words, and these few words embrace the principles of the moral law as designed for the whole world. To this day they form the basis of all moral law and obligation, and the ethics and the laws of the world are perfect and effective, just in proportion as they accept and develop and guard these foundation-principles of duty and justice to God and man as laid down in the ten commandments.

The fourth of these commandments reads, "Remember the Sabbath day to keep it holy. Six days shalt thou labor and do all thy work, but the seventh day is the Sabbath of the Lord thy God. In it thou shalt not do any work, thou nor thy son, nor thy daughter, thy man-servant nor thy maid-servant, nor thy cattle, nor thy stranger that is within thy gates, for in six days the Lord made heaven and earth, the sea and all that in them is, and rested the seventh day, wherefore the Lord blessed the Sabbath day and hallowed it." Ex. xx. 8–11. This was the formal proclamation of the Sabbatic law. It is embedded in a divine code not one provision of which has been abrogated or set aside.

It should be observed that in the very enacting of this law of the Sabbath the divine Lawgiver traces it back to its origin in his own rest on the seventh day, deduces from that the reason for its perpetual and universal observance, and is the only one of the ten commandments for which an historic reason is assigned.

This law has never been abrogated; the day has been changed, but the obligation to set apart a seventh portion of time as hallowed time still holds, and will hold till the end of time.

Under the Jewish economy the law of the Sabbath involved several points. In the twenty-third chapter of the book of Leviticus we find this law incorporated into the statutes of the Jewish theocracy, with certain added prescriptions designed to show how it was to be kept holy. There it stands at the head of that chapter wherein are officially declared by Moses, acting by express command of God, what shall be the "feasts of the Lord" and "the holy convocations" of his people Israel. "Six days shall work be done, but the seventh day is the

Sabbath of rest, a holy convocation; it is the Sabbath of the Lord in all your dwellings." This is the ordinance of the Sabbath as found in the Jewish statute-book, the book of Leviticus. Like the law of Sinai, it enjoins six days of labor and a seventh day of rest. In addition to this positive command it requires two things—that this Sabbath shall be "a holy convocation," and that it shall be kept "in all your dwellings." From the Sinaitic law and the Levitical statute we gather these elemental and obligatory points. The Sabbath was to be *a rest* day; it was to be the *seventh* day; it was to be a *holy* day; it was to be a day of *holy convocation*, or the assembling of people for holy purposes; and it was to be kept *in every family and dwelling*. God distinctly declared (Ex. xxxi. 16, 17), "Wherefore the children of Israel shall keep the Sabbath, to observe the Sabbath throughout their generations, for a perpetual covenant. It is a sign between me and the children of Israel for ever." The penalty of death was affixed to the breaking of the Sabbath: "Every one that defileth it shall surely be put to death, for whosoever doeth any work therein, that soul shall be cut off from among his people." These facts prove the truth of the remark that "there was no rite nor institution, not even circumcision, by which the Jews were more conspicuously distinguished from surrounding nations and marked off as the worshipers of Jehovah, the Creator of the ends of the earth. Their Sabbath-keeping was a perpetual and visible token of the connection in which they stood to God, and of the great mission which under him they were set apart to discharge." It was the sign between God and his people—the sign of the covenant; so that to break the Sabbath was to break the covenant with God.

Aside from these general regulations, there were no specific directions as to how the Sabbath should be spent. There was in the earlier days of the Jewish Church no prescribed religious observance for this day, except that the daily sacrifices were to be doubled and the loaves of shew-bread on the table in the holy place were to be renewed by twelve fresh cakes.

It was a day of sacred festivity, of social gathering, of religious instruction, of personal freedom, of physical rest for man and beast. As the nation grew in wealth and luxury, as they imbibed by the very process of contact evil habits and thoughts from the surrounding heathen nations, as amidst their own tribal rivalries and internecine wars laxity of morals grew apace, so the law of the Sabbath, like the other laws of God, became gradually neglected and profaned. Work encroached little by little on rest, secularity usurped the place of devotion; and though one prophet after another was raised up to warn the people, yet the defection went on until the captivity engulfed priest and people and sacrifices and Sabbaths in one overwhelming sorrow and chastisement. They had polluted his Sabbaths and broken his covenant, and hence God gave them for a time into the hands of their enemies. After their return under Nehemiah a stricter observance was enforced. The lessons learned in the captivity were severe but wholesome. The temporary expatriation had brought with it great searchings of heart, and these had resulted in great resolutions of amendment of life. As they sat by the rivers of Babylon they looked back to their once quiet Sabbaths and holy convocations as to fading visions of delight.

As their harps hung silent upon the willows they called to mind their joyous festivals and seventh-day gladness; and thus thrown in upon themselves, and made to bend their minds upon the inner blessings of the land and the covenant which they had to all appearance lost, they saw the greatness of their loss, and mourned in bitterness of spirit their expatriation from Judea and the destruction of their holy temple. It was after the captivity that the Schools of the Rabbis were founded and the sect of the Pharisees established. The laxity of former times was now offset by extreme rigidity. A spirit of intense Judaism was fostered by the Scribes and Pharisees. The law of Moses was overlaid with the incrustations of rabbinic traditions. The teachings of the elders were only instilling into the minds of learners the punctilious observance of human commandments engrafted on the divine, until at last the parasitic commandments overshadowed the original law of God, sucked out its real strength, and substituted that which was human and illegal, for that which was legal and divine.

This spirit finds its record in the Mishna and the Gemmara, and in the Talmud, the common and post-Christian repository of all the exactions, sayings, traditions, puerilities and extravagances of the great Jewish schools and the doctors of the Jewish law. The pharisaic party, in their zeal to tone up the long-relaxed popular mind, and to reinstate the almost practically abolished Sabbath, did that which degraded rather than exalted it, and "made it the object of an idolatrous regard, the central figure in a religion wholly ceremonial." Its primary injunction, "Thou shalt do no manner of work," was falsely held as aimed at all kinds of work whatever, no less than thirty-nine kinds or classes of work being specified as involved in the prohibition. Thus it was stated that grass was not to be trodden on on the Sabbath, for the bruising of it was a species of harvest work. A man might fill a trough with water for beasts to come to, but might not carry water to them. To eat an egg laid on the first day of the week was interdicted because presumably it was prepared in the order of nature on the seventh or Sabbath day. Shoes with nails were not to be worn on that day, as that was the carrying of a burden; and according to one school of teaching, it was not only not lawful to heal on the Sabbath day, but it was wrong even to minister to the sick. It was also laid down in the Mishna that when the sun begins to darken a tailor must not walk out with his needle lest sunset should overtake him carrying it. Nor may a scribe walk out with his inkhorn and pen lest he forget and go with it in his hand. After the Sabbath lamp is lighted one must not begin to pick vermin from his clothes, nor yet begin to read by its light, for that would be servile work. These Sabbatic laws, in all their burdensome minuteness and frivolousness, were an essential part of Judaism. It has been truly said, "They burden the conscience of the sincere and make the unscrupulous hypocrites." "For to keep the rabbinical Sabbath aright it is necessary to be perfectly acquainted with all the laws relating to it, which are very many and very intricate, occupying above one hundred and seventy folio pages."

Maimonides and Kimchi, fathers of the traditions, in a gloss upon the words of Isaiah (lviii. 13), "Thou shalt call the Sabbath a delight," say, "It is forbidden to fast on the Sabbath, but on the contrary men are bound to delight themselves with meat and drink, for we must live more delicately on the Sabbath than other days, and he is highly to be commended who provides the most delicious junkets against that day. We must eat thrice on the Sabbath, and all men are to be admonished of it; and even the poor themselves, who live on alms, let them eat thrice on the Sabbath, for he that feasts thrice on the Sabbath shall be delivered from the calamities of the Messiah, from the judgment of hell and from the war of Gog and Magog."

This is an instance—and they might be indefinitely multiplied—where, starting from a true principle that the Sabbath was to be a delight and not a day of dull austerity, they run out their interpretations into most ridiculous details, the usual style of rabbinical theology stretching the literal interpretation to the perversion, and subversion often, of the true spirit and intent of the law. "Under the shadow of the traditions the most palpable illegalities could be with impunity committed, and even, on occasions, the literal meaning of one ordinance could be played off against another so that both should be rendered futile."

Such are a specimen of the absurdities and excesses which the pharisaic party ran into in their attempt to throw guards and restrictions around the fourth commandment. Missing to a great extent its inner spirit, they legislated for its outward observance. Led on by a line of false interpretation which made no allowance for change of times and circumstances, and which looked fixedly and solely to the letter of the command, they were led by their inexorable logic to the conclusions which we have stated. They erected cheval-de-frise around that law, bristling with a hundred points, upon any one of which the incautious and unwary would impale himself. They made this law the first and great commandment, the keeping of it superior in its sanctity to all the others, and declared that he who kept the Sabbath holy—holy in their sense—would merit salvation even if he broke every other command in the Decalogue. Thus they made the word of God of none effect through their traditions, and they taught for divine doctrine the commandments of men.

"You remember and admire," says Coleridge, "the saying of an old divine that ceremony duly initiated is a chain of gold around the neck of faith; but if in the wish to make it co-essential and consubstantial you draw it closer and closer, it may strangle the faith it was made to deck and designate." This is what the Scribes and Pharisees did to the Sabbath. They strangled it with the chains of excessive exactions and directions. Its true life, vigor, breadth, glory, was gone in the tightening of those ligatures which they fastened around its neck, designedly for its more comely adornment, but resulting in the eventual destruction of the ordinance in its true import as established by God.

It is important to bear these things in mind in studying the acts of our Lord on the Sabbath day. Much of the force of his teaching and of his example is lost if we are ignorant of the peculiar aspect of the Sabbath question in his day.

We find him on no less than seven different occasions working miracles of healing on that day and justifying himself to the carping Pharisees by saying, "My Father worketh hitherto, and I work." We notice him every now and then animadverting upon their glosses and traditions as exalting the "letter of the law, which killeth," above "its spirit, which giveth life."

Coming, as Jesus did, "not to destroy the law,

but to fulfill" it, it was necessary that he should first recover the law from the manipulations of its professed friends—that he should let it be seen what it originally was, and what it was meant for, and how it was to be kept. To this end, he removed the additions which age after age had been added to the divine statute until at last, what men had enacted, covered up what God had ordained.

Like everything else which he touched, Jesus put this law in its true position and light. He rescued it from the hands of the scribes and Pharisees, and showed it as God would have us esteem it, a day of holy rest, holy service and merciful works. It was God the Son commenting by word and deed upon the law of God the Father. And God the Holy Ghost has inspired holy men of old to write out these teachings and incidents:—and thus we have the threefold testimony of the triune God to the true nature and blessedness of the patriarchal, the Mosaic and the Christian Sabbath.

NAZARETH.

THE SABBATHS OF OUR LORD.

CHAPTER I.

THE FIRST SABBATH AT NAZARETH.

"And he came to Nazareth, where he had been brought up: and, as his custom was, he went into the synagogue on the Sabbath day, and stood up for to read. And there was delivered unto him the book of the prophet Esaias. And when he had opened the book, he found the place where it was written, The Spirit of the Lord is upon me, because he hath anointed me to preach the Gospel to the poor; he hath sent me to heal the broken-hearted, to preach deliverance to the captives, and recovering of sight to the blind, to set at liberty them that are bruised, to preach the acceptable year of the Lord. And he closed the book, and he gave *it* again to the minister, and sat down. And the eyes of all them that were in the synagogue were fastened on him. And he began to say unto them, This day is this Scripture fulfilled in your ears. And all bare him witness, and wondered at the gracious words which proceeded out of his mouth. And they said, Is not this Joseph's son? And he said unto them, Ye will surely say unto me this proverb, Physician, heal thyself: whatsoever we have heard done in Capernaum, do also here in thy country. And he said, Verily I say unto you, No prophet is accepted in his own country. But I tell you of a truth, many widows were in Israel in the days of Elias, when the heaven was shut up three years and six months, when great famine was throughout all the land; but unto none of them was Elias sent, save unto Sarepta, *a city* of Sidon, unto a woman *that was* a widow. And many lepers were in Israel in the time of Eliseus the prophet; and none of them was cleansed, saving Naaman the Syrian. And all they in the synagogue, when they heard these things, were filled with wrath, and rose up, and thrust him out of the city, and led him unto the brow of the hill whereon their city was built, that they might cast him down headlong. But he passing through the midst of them went his way, and came down to Capernaum, a city of Galilee, and taught them on the Sabbath days." LUKE IV. 16–31.

WE shall speak of this Sabbath first, because in his teachings on this day our Lord opened before us his whole work and mission as the Messiah. The Evangelist says, "*He came to Nazareth,*" implying that he had been away, and so he had. When he became thirty years old, the Levitical age at which only a man could take upon himself the office of a priest, he left Nazareth, and we find him visiting John the Baptist, who was preaching "the baptism of repentance for the remission of sins" on the banks of the river Jordan, and thus fulfilling his office as "the voice of one crying in the wilderness, Prepare ye the way of the Lord."

Here, and by his own "Forerunner," he was baptized, for thus "it became him to fulfill all righteousness." Here, as he went up from the river's brink, "he saw the heavens opened, and the Spirit of God descending like a dove and lighting upon him, and lo a voice from heaven saying, This is my beloved Son in whom I am well pleased."

From this baptismal scene he was "led up of the Spirit into the wilderness to be tempted of the devil." In this wilderness (whether it be the desert between the Mount of Olives and Jericho, called Quarantania, as some suppose, or the desert of Arabia, as is believed by others) he fasted "forty days and forty nights." From this wilderness, having first overcome the devil in his threefold temptation by the sword of the Spirit, which is the word of God, he departed into Galilee and went to Nazareth, "where he had been brought up." Were it not that everything connected with our Lord's birth and earthly life is a marvel, and goes contrary to man's preconceived opinions, we should wonder that so obscure a place as Nazareth should be selected as the place of his longest earthly sojourn. It is not once mentioned in the Old Testament, nor by the Jewish historian Josephus, nor do we find any record of its existence until it is spoken of as the home of the Virgin Mary. The name is derived from the Hebrew word Netser or "branch," and means the "city of branches," and the Holy Spirit teaches us that by growing up at Nazareth, the city of branches, He whose name is "The Branch" thus fulfilled the spirit of the ancient prophecies of Isaiah (xi. 1), Jeremiah (xxiii. 5) and Zechariah (iii. 8), which St. Matthew has condensed into the phrase "he shall be called a Nazarene."

In the turbulent district of Lower Galilee, and in the province given to the tribe of Zebulon, lies this now famous town. According to the rate of travel in that country, it is a three days' journey from Jerusalem, being about sixty-five miles north of it.

After crossing the plain of Esdraelon, so celebrated for centuries as the battlefield of many of the most warlike nations of the world, from the times of Deborah and Sisera down to the last year of the last century, when Bonaparte obtained there a signal victory over the Turks, you ascend the hills which constitute the southern ridges of the Lebanon range, and winding among them in their picturesque beauty for a little while, you then gradually descend into Nazareth. It lies in a beautiful sequestered nook in the midst of fertile slopes and valleys, and its gardens abound with the olive, the fig and the pomegranate trees, and altogether presents a pleasing and thrifty appearance.

Here it was, more than eighteen centuries ago, that the angel Gabriel came, when sent from God, "to a virgin espoused to a man whose name was Joseph of the house of David," to tell this "handmaid of the Lord," "Fear not, Mary, for thou hast found favor with God, and behold thou shalt conceive in thy womb and bring forth a son, and thou shalt call his name Jesus."

Here it was, when Joseph "was minded to put her away privily" because "she was found with child of the Holy Ghost," that the angel of the Lord appeared unto him in a dream, saying, "Joseph, thou son of David, fear not to take unto thee Mary thy wife, for that which is conceived in her is of the Holy Ghost." Here it was that Joseph and Mary were united in marriage by the striking forms of the Hebrew ritual after this visit of the angel, having previously and before the annunciation of Gabriel been publicly betrothed to each other, and from that betrothal were in law, though not in fact, regarded as "man and wife."

Here it was, after the birth of Christ and their temporary flight into Egypt to avoid the cruelty of Herod, and the fear created in their minds by the reign of his son Archelaus, that the humble couple and the child Jesus took up their abode in peace and seclusion.

Here it was that Joseph toiled in daily labor at the trade of a village carpenter, and Mary, watching the growth of the infant Saviour, pondering all these things in her heart, did the duties of a housewife.

From this place it was that Joseph and Mary and Jesus, when the latter was twelve years old, went up to Jerusalem, because Jesus was now a Hebrew catechumen, a "child of the law," or "of the precept," as they were termed, and all such, according to the usages of the Jewish Church, were to be catechised by the elders and scribes.

To this place the parents and "child Jesus" returned after this wonderful visit to Jerusalem, when Jesus was found "in the temple sitting in the midst of the doctors, both hearing them and asking them questions," causing all to be "astonished at his understanding and answers."

Here it was, at a later period, that, in accordance with the requirements of Jewish law which demanded that every male child should learn some trade, Jesus learned his reputed father's trade and wrought as a carpenter among the townspeople of Nazareth. Here it was that he "grew in wisdom and in stature, and in favor with God and man."

Thus, from the time that he was two years old until he reached the age of thirty, Jesus dwelt in Nazareth, passing more than five-sixths of the time in which he tabernacled in the flesh in this notedly despised town of Galilee, for that Nazareth was looked down upon as a low and immoral place is evident from the question which that "Israelite indeed," Nathanael, asked, when in reply to the words of Philip concerning Jesus he said, "Can there any good thing come out of Nazareth?"

What in the history or character of the people of that town gave rise to that proverbial expression of Nathanael we do not know. "By the figure which they make in the Evangelist," says Doddridge, "they seem to have deserved it;" and is it not another instance of the voluntary humility of our Lord that instead of spending his infancy and youth and early manhood in a quiet, peaceful town, amid the gentler virtues of a rural people, he tarried in turbulent Galilee and found his longest home among the rude, ill-mannered, vindictive and jealous Nazarethites?

How much of interest thus clusters about

Nazareth! and how much scope does the imagination find in picturing out the childhood and manhood, the home-life and the town-life, the school days and the apprentice days of Jesus of Nazareth! It has a period of twenty-eight years to revel in, and can roam over all the changes and fluctuations of life, from the two-year-old prattler at his mother's knee to the matured man of thirty, just starting out on his divine mission to be the Saviour of the world. Our visit to Nazareth was one of singular interest. We entered it from the south, and skirting the edge of the town, rode on to its end, where, under the shade of a grove of olive trees and close to a beautiful spring, we pitched our tents and found refreshment after the hot and weary ride across the plain of Esdraelon. This fountain is the most voluminous in the town, and from it the women take most of the water that is drunk in it. It is called "The fountain of the virgin," not only, and with great probability, because the mother of Jesus often, like most of the maidens of Nazareth, resorted thither to draw water and bear it away in water-jars on their heads or shoulders, as we saw hundreds doing, but especially because, according to the traditions of the Greek Church, it was while Mary was at this spring that the angel Gabriel met her and announced that she should be the mother of the Messiah. Accordingly, to commemorate this supposed event, the Greek Church has built near by the "Convent of the Annunciation." The Latin Church, on the other hand, says that the "annunciation" took place, not at the spring, but in the house of Mary, and points to the grottoes or chambers in the Franciscan church of the chapel of the Annunciation as part of her dwelling. The droning monks pretend to show you the window through which the angel Gabriel flew, and the column which the empress Helena placed to mark the spot where Mary stood or knelt at the time of the angelic visit.

Nothing could more surely destroy the truthfulness of the monks' story than the fact asserted by Romish writers; that about the thirteenth century a band of angels took up bodily the house of Mary in Nazareth, then threatened with desecration, and bearing it through the air across the Mediterranean and up the Adriatic gulf, set it down first at Rimini and then on a hill called Loretto. There the so-called "*Casa*

Santa," "the House of Our Lady of Loretto," now stands, an object of deepest veneration and superstition to the devout of the Romish Church. The walls of this house of "Our Lady" are externally covered with marble, a gorgeous temple has been built up over it, a hundred priests minister in it, a hundred and twenty-three masses are daily said in its precincts. Jewels and vessels of gold and silver, and gorgeous tapestry, and services of various kinds, enrich the shrine, and the pavement around the house is literally worn with the knees of peasants and priests and prelates and princes, as they for centuries have crawled devoutly around it. Here also, in this marble-encased cabin, is shown the window through which Gabriel came—here also the spot where the Virgin heard the angelic "Ave Maria;" and as if this did not sufficiently tax the credulity of the faithful, you are also shown, in this same "Casa Santa," the altar where St. Peter first said mass after our Lord's ascension, when the apostles met at Nazareth, and turned this house into a church.

Leaving the Church which fosters these superstitions to reconcile their discrepancies, we turn away from these lying wonders to the lovely valley which stretches away to the east and south of the town, to the numerous hills which environ it like a girdle, to the babbling stream which marks its way by its green borders through the edge of the town, and picture before us, as far as imagination permits, the childhood, boyhood and early manhood of Jesus as they were here displayed to the rustic Nazarethites.

It was most thrilling to be there. Du Saulcy says that "he wept as he stood in the chapel of the Annunciation," and other travelers have recorded their deep emotions as they heard therein the pealing organ and the solemn chants of the priests. These constitute no attraction for the true Christian, but they are moved, moved to tears and prayers, as they walk up and down those hills, over those plains, down by the fountain and across the fields, studded with clumps of olive and fig trees, and tesselated with the flowers of God's arranging, because every spot seems full of the memories of Jesus. How often had he walked over these fields! how often followed his mother to the fountain! how often climbed those hills! how often gone up there for retirement and prayer! how often, as he stood upon their tops, had he looked northward to the snow-crowned head of Hermon, eastward to the rounded top of Tabor, southward across the plain of Esdraelon to the mountains of Gilboa and Benjamin, and westward to the promontory of Carmel, where Elijah slew the prophets of Baal, as it jutted out into the great sea!

The twenty-eight years' life of Jesus in this spot have consecrated the town and its surroundings and made it hallowed ground.

Yet the whole authentic record of these years is contained in the verses (Luke ii. 40): "And the child grew and waxed strong in spirit, filled with wisdom, and the grace of God was upon him;" and after his return from Jerusalem, whither at twelve years of age he had gone to the feast of the Passover, it is said (Luke ii. 51, 52), "And he went down with them and came to Nazareth, and was subject unto them, and Jesus increased in wisdom and stature, and in favor with God and man." This is all the record that we have of his long residence in Nazareth.

Marvelous silence! The prying curiosity of men would fain know how our Lord looked as a babe, how he played as a boy, how he mingled with his companions, how he wrought as a carpenter, how he behaved as a young man in society, how the people of Nazareth regarded him, with a hundred other questions about matters where the Bible is silent.

What should we say of human biographers who should thus skip over four-fifths of the lives of the subjects of their writings, who should tell us nothing of the childhood, the appearance, the habits of person or of mind, the education and associations, of the one whose life they were portraying? It would be strange and unsatisfactory. But this silence of the Scripture in reference to our Lord is deeply instructive, and even with our finite minds we can see its wisdom. We desire to know the infancy and childhood of earthly heroes, in order that we may mark the causes, and trace the development, of those traits of mind and heart for which they afterward became renowned, and thus observe the mental and moral processes by which their character was built up and compacted into historic greatness. But our Lord was beholden to no such parental or domestic training, to no such social or educational influences; and hence there was no necessity to tell the occurrences of his early life as the clew or key to his subsequent history, for it was not moulded by earthly surroundings, nor did human teachers give shape and direction to his mental or moral powers. His childhood ever blossomed with the beauty of holiness, his boyhood was ever fragrant with the expanding flowers of grace, and his manhood brought forth day by day the ripened fruit of the Spirit, for it is emphatically said, "The child grew and waxed strong in spirit, filled with wisdom, and the grace of God was upon him."

There is also something sublime in this silence of Scripture, for instead of leading off our thoughts to the early life of Jesus, and thus diffusing our interest over all the years that he tabernacled in the flesh, the Holy Ghost now concentrates all our looks and feelings on the one work which it was the one object of his life to accomplish. He thus rebukes a prurient curiosity, and rejects as useless what is not immediately connected with redemption. The sacred writers are here dealing with the most marvelous deeds and the most astounding works of grace, and they cannot stop to tell the doings of years which had no immediate relation to his work as Prophet, Priest and King; of years which were but the temporal links which connected the cross of Calvary with the manger of Bethlehem, and the virgin-born Son of Mary with the risen and ascended Lord of glory.

As we contemplate this reticence of Scripture, how forcibly are we impressed with the sublime truth, "It is the glory of God to conceal a thing"! Infinite wisdom, checking the else rampant imagination of man, has made a biographical blank where men would have written minute histories, but we know that the blank will be filled up by and by, and we must be content to wait until we see Jesus in heaven and "follow him whithersoever he goeth" to learn the real history of his abode at Nazareth.

5

CHAPTER II.

THE FIRST SABBATH AT NAZARETH.
(Continued.)

WE said that we had no records of our Lord's doings at Nazareth until he appears on this Sabbath in the synagogue. This is true as to positive records, yet we have in the passage which describes this Sabbath four words—"as his custom was"—which give us some insight into his previous character, and by inference at least tells us what his Sabbath habits were. The whole sentence reads, "And as his custom was, he went into the synagogue on the Sabbath day and stood up for to read." That word, "custom," carries us away back to his childhood. We see him as a child, led by his mother's hand, walking to the synagogue week after week, taking his place as a child, or as a catechumen, with the other "children of the precept," reverently listening to the reading of the law and the prophets.

We see him, as he arrives at man's estate, still going every seventh day to the same synagogue and taking his part in its simple services. This he doubtless did always.

He did not plead as a reason why he should remain away, that that worship had become corrupt—that they had made the word of God "of none effect through their traditions," their glosses and their false interpretations.

Nor did he, in the conscious holiness of his own soul, feeling that he needed not this human instrumentality for his own perfection, neglect it, and thus throw the force of his example against it, by forsaking the assembling of himself with others on that sacred day. This habitual attendance of our Lord on divine worship is a guide and model to us; for if the holy Jesus could tolerate all the imperfections of synagogue worship in the degenerate days in which he lived, conducted by the scribes and Pharisees, who were so polluted and hypocritical as they were in his day, then surely ought we to gather ourselves within the courts of the Lord's house, and not stay away because of personal antipathies to minister or people, hypercritical objections to pulpit teaching, hypocritical assumptions of religious superiority, or alleged defects, or excesses, in the mode of worship.

As we shall often have occasion to speak of the synagogues, it may be well here to give a general description of them, in order the better to understand the allusions which will be so frequently made.

"Synagogue" is a Greek word employed in the Septuagint as the translation of twenty-one Hebrew words in which the idea of a gathering is implied, and means literally, a meeting-house.

Though many Jewish writers claim for the Synagogue a very remote antiquity, yet its real origin does not date, probably, earlier than the days of Ezra after the return of the Jews from Babylonish exile. Then we have distinct traces of what has been called "the synagogue parochial system," both among the Jews in Palestine and in other countries. According to the Talmudists, wherever ten families lived, there a Synagogue was to be erected, though generally but one was built in each town. Their structure was simple, and varied with the tastes and wealth of the congregation. Usually they were erected on the highest ground in or near the city, and were so arranged that as the worshiper entered and bowed, his face was "toward Jerusalem," where was the one only temple and the one only sacrifice. In the prayer of consecration offered by King Solomon on the occasion of dedicating the Temple which he had built to the worship of almighty God, he again and again speaks of "praying toward this house," of spreading forth his hands "toward this house," of praying "toward this place, the city which thou hast chosen and the house which I have built for thy name," and thus indicates the posture and direction which the Israelite would take, in whatsoever land he abode, when he sought to worship the God of his fathers. The internal construction of the Synagogue was symbolical of the temple. At the upper or Jerusalem end, stood the ark, the chest which, like the older and more sacred ark, contained the book of the law. It gave to that end the name and character of a sanctuary. This part of the Synagogue was naturally the place of honor. Here were the "chief seats," for which Pharisees and scribes strove so eagerly, and to which the wealthy and honored worshiper was invited. Here too, in front of the ark, still reproducing the type of the tabernacle, was the eight-branched lamp lighted only on the greater festivals. Beside these there was one lamp kept burning perpetually. A little farther toward the middle of the building was a raised platform on which several persons could stand at once, and in the middle of this rose a pulpit in which the reader stood to read the lesson or sat down to teach. The congregation was divided, the men on one side, the women on the other, a low partition five or six feet high running between them. The arrangement of modern synagogues, for many centuries, has made the separation more complete by placing the women in low side galleries screened off by lattice-work.

The officers of the Synagogue were, first, the "ruler" or chief of the Synagogue, who exercised rectorial care over the building and the people, then the "elders," or heads of the Synagogue, then the "reader," or legate, who blended the office of a reader, secretary and messenger, then the "minister," or attendant, who opened the doors, prepared the place for service, took the sacred rolls from the ark and gave them to the reader, and receiving them again, replaced them in their sanctuary. The worship of the synagogue was made up of fixed forms of prayer (each chief ruler being authorized to make such for his own synagogue), the reading of the law and the prophets in such consecutive order as that the whole should-be read through in a cycle of three years, and in an exposition by some one of the worshipers of the portion of Scripture previously read.

The Hebrew Church divided the "law," or Pentateuch, into fifty-four sections (parashahs), or proper lessons, which were read in the synagogues on the Sabbath. To these were added proper lessons (haphtarahs) taken out of the prophets, and they were coupled together in a calendar directing when they were to be read.

Thus the first section (parashah) of the Pentateuch began with the first chapter of Genesis and extended to the eighth verse of the sixth chapter, "But Noah found grace in the eyes of the Lord." The corresponding prophetical lesson (haphtarah) is taken from Isaiah xlii. 5–21, and we note at once the parallelism between them, as both refer to the work of creation. This is something like the first and second lessons in the calendar of the Protestant Episcopal Church, only in this Church the second lesson is taken out of the New Testament, so as to make the two testaments or covenants, the Mosaic and the Christian, reflect light on each other, for there is no interpreter of Scripture so good and so exact as Scripture itself, whereby we may compare "spiritual things with spiritual."

Several features of the Christian Church have been evidently borrowed from the forms of the Synagogue. This is not to be wondered at when we consider that the apostles were educated in the usages of the Synagogue, and that it was by means of the synagogues planted by the Jewish colonies in various parts of the world that the gospel was introduced to the Hebrew and the Gentile nations, for into whatever country the apostles went, they usually found there a synagogue, and thither they resorted, and in it first preached salvation through Jesus Christ. Thus God had providentially prepared these reading and preaching places, these depositories of the law and the prophets, these houses of Sabbatical worship and assembling, as so many *foci* in which to gather the religious elements of the age, and from which to shed forth the glo-

"And he went down with them and came to Nazareth, and was subject unto them."

rious light of the gospel of Jesus Christ, "of whom Moses in the law and the prophets did write."

In addition to religious uses, the synagogue was also the common school of the village, where the children were taught by the Rabbi the elements of education, and who especially grounded them in the knowledge of the law and the more noted traditions of the elders. It was doubtless in one of these synagogue schools that our Lord learned the rudiments of Jewish learning.

Another function which the Synagogue fulfilled was that of a court of justice. It was the town court. Its rulers were as justices of the peace. Trials of minor cases were held there, and the adjudged punishment of scourging was often administered there, and our Lord distinctly warns his disciples that among other ill treatment "they will scourge you in their synagogues."

Thus learning, law, religion, clustered around the Synagogue and made it the centre of the most potent influences that can mould a community.

There was generally a desk on which the rolls

of parchment were placed, so that, as one side of the sacred Scriptures was unrolled, the other side could be conveniently rolled up, for the books of that day were not made into leaves like ours, but were mostly of skins rolled into convenient size and labeled on the outside and secured by a leathern clasp or thong. In reading these rolls of the law and the prophets, the reader always " stood up," imitating the position of Ezra in his " pulpit of wood" in the streets of Jerusalem, and the practice of the Jewish assemblies from the rebuilding of the temple. Some have thought that the phrase, "As his custom was," refers not to his habit of going every Sabbath to the Synagogue, but to the being frequently called upon to read out of the holy rolls. It may be so, for sometimes the reader was one of the assembly who was neither an office-bearer, or a scribe or Pharisee, and sometimes, also, the expounder of the law was even a stranger, as in the case of the Synagogue at Antioch, where, after the reading of the prophets, St. Luke says, "The rulers of the Synagogue sent unto Paul and his companions, saying, Ye men and brethren, if ye have any word of exhortation for the people, say on."

Being a general favorite with the people (for it is said that "he grew in favor with God and man"), and perhaps from his ability to read the Scriptures with more truthfulness of expression because he knew, as they did not, the deep meaning of each word and sentence, Jesus was probably often called upon to "stand up for to read." Little did that simple folk imagine who it was that read to them such weighty words. They saw in him only a good young man of spotless life and devout habits, a well-beloved citizen and industrious mechanic; in fine, an Israelite in whom there was no guile. They did not know that there was standing in their midst the *Seed* of the woman who was "to bruise the serpent's head," the "*Prophet* greater than Moses," the "*Messiah*" of whom David so royally sung, the "*Prince of peace*" of whom Isaiah prophesied, the "*Son of man*" seen in the visions of the holy Daniel, the "*Lord*" who, according to Malachi, was so suddenly to come to his temple. The veil was upon their eyes and upon their hearts; their mental vision was as yet not prepared for such an outburst of glory; but the long looked-for "day-star" was now to arise, and the ears of that Sabbath assembly were to be startled that morning by an announcement that would fill them with excitement and wonder, for as "he stood up for to read," "there was delivered unto him (by the one whose office it was to fetch and carry back the rolls from the sanctuary) the book (or roll) of the prophet Esaias (Isaiah), and when he had opened the book he found the place where it was written—Isaiah lxi. 1.—'The Spirit of the Lord is upon me, because he hath anointed me to preach the gospel to the poor; he hath sent me to heal the brokenhearted, to preach deliverance to the captives and recovering of sight to the blind, to set at liberty them that are bruised, to preach the acceptable year of the Lord.' And he closed the book and gave it again unto the minister and sat down, and the eyes of all them that were in the Synagogue were fastened on him, and he began to say unto them, This day is this scripture fulfilled in your ears." A murmur of surprise rises from the assembly and glances of wonder pass from eye to eye at this bold declaration, but soon they hush themselves into silence that they may listen more attentively to the Carpenter who now for the first time preaches in their Synagogue.

CHAPTER III.

THE FIRST SABBATH AT NAZARETH.
(Continued.)

LET us in imagination seat ourselves in the Synagogue of Nazareth and listen to "the gracious words" which proceed out of the mouth of Jesus.

It is all the more interesting because it is the record of the only time our Lord read in the synagogue, and also of the first sermon which he preached; because by taking his text from Isaiah he endorsed the inspiration of that evangelical prophet; and especially because in this his first discourse among his neighbors and kinsfolk, "where he had been brought up," he expounds the character of the Messiah, and the nature of the kingdom which he was anointed to establish.

On comparing the words of St. Luke with

those of Isaiah we find some slight verbal differences, owing, doubtless, to the fact that, while our Lord read from and expounded the pure Hebrew words as written by Isaiah, St. Luke, who wrote his gospel for the Hellenist Jews, quotes from the Septuagint version of that prophet, as one with which they were more familiar. The differences, however, are only verbal, and of no exegetical value. The grand thought is the same, and it is with the thought itself, rather than with its drapery of words, that we have now to do.

Of what our Lord said upon this passage of Isaiah we have but one sentence preserved, viz.: "This day is this Scripture fulfilled in your ears." In what manner he applied this prophecy to himself, and how he unfolded its inner meaning, we know not. That it was done with an unction and earnestness which they had never before seen is evident from the statement of St. Luke that all "wondered at the gracious words which proceeded out of his lips." As their fellow-townsman opened to them this Scripture, fitting to his own person and office the several parts of this prophecy, bringing out of the sacred text a hidden meaning which their wisest scribes had never taught, and making clear as the sunlight what had so long been obscured by mists of traditions received from their fathers, the people, we can imagine, sat in mute astonishment and awe. They gave him their undivided attention; they let not a word fall to the ground, but recognized to a certain extent their grace and power.

To understand this the better, let us see what this prophecy required for its fulfillment, and then ascertain whether He who then spake met these conditions.

This prophecy of Isaiah was regarded by all the Jews as referring to the advent of the Messiah. It demanded, first, that the person fulfilling it should be the Messiah or *anointed* one, for the words, "Messiah" in Hebrew, "Christos" in Greek, are equivalent to the English, Christ or anointed. Anointing was one of the solemn forms of setting apart prophets, priests and kings. But the anointed one of the text was to be set apart, not with material oil, as were Elisha and Aaron and David, but by the Spirit of the Lord God—*i.e.*, by the outpouring or descent of the Holy Ghost; and was not Jesus thus anointed when the Holy Ghost like a dove lighted upon him at his baptism in Jordan? It required, secondly, that this "anointed one" should be a Prophet preaching glad tidings, preaching the gospel, preaching "the acceptable year of the Lord." Did not Jesus go up and down Judea preaching the word, and so speaking that not only did he draw multitudes to his discourses, but the very soldiers who were sent to apprehend him returned, saying, "Never man spake like this man"? He was, of a truth, "that Prophet" greater than Moses which the Lord God was to raise up to his people Israel.

It required, thirdly, that this "anointed one" should be able to stay the effect of sin in whatsoever form that sin manifested itself. Thus, as the prophecy intimated, he was to "heal," or "bind up," the broken-hearted, those whom sin had crushed and made sad and trampled under foot. He was to preach "deliverance to the captives"—the captives of Satan, the victims of his snares and arts. He was "to give sight to the blind," those who were spiritually as well as physically blind, and who could not see the things which pertained to their eternal peace. He was to "set at liberty them that are bruised"— bruised under the yoke and burden of sin, manacled and galled by the fetters of the prince of darkness, whose bond-slaves they were. Did not Jesus do all this both to the bodies and the souls of men in the miracles of mercy which he wrought, and in the effect of the doctrines which he taught? and is it not the special purpose of his religion to achieve for the mind, for the heart, for the bodies of men, for man individually and men collectively, in families, states, churches, nations, exactly those things which are here predicted? Thus he rolls back the effects of sin as it causes woe and darkness and captivity and oppression and every evil work.

It required, fourthly, that this "anointed one" should restore to man the inheritance which he had lost in Eden. The term "to preach the acceptable year of the Lord" refers to that joyful day and year when, according to the directions given in Leviticus, at the close of each forty-ninth year, the priests, on the morning which ushered in the fiftieth year, were to "blow the silver trumpets of the jubilee and proclaim liberty throughout all the land and unto all the inhabitants thereof"—trumpet notes heard seldom more than once in a lifetime, but when heard, they filled the heart of the nation with an exuberance of joy that found its outburst in all manner of festive gladness and thanksgiving. And why this gladness? Because then, a year of rest was proclaimed, and there was neither ploughing nor sowing nor reaping, but the land itself had a Sabbatical year. Because then, every Israelite recovered his right and title to the land originally allotted to his ancestors, and the alienated inheritance was his again without purchase. Because then, the bondmen went out free from servitude and were restored to their original franchise, and thus there was given back to each Israelite his covenanted right and portion in the land of promise given to him by Jehovah.

This year of jubilee, occurring after each seven weeks of years, or forty-nine years, was typical of the triumph of the Messiah when he would restore to man his lost inheritance, when he would set him free from the bondage under which sin had enslaved him, when he would dispense to all "the rest," the jubilee rest, "which remaineth for the people of God."

And is not this what Christ is now doing, and will still further do, as the jubilee sound of the gospel trumpet goes out into all lands and wakes up notes of joy and salvation among all the tribes and races of men? The inheritance which we lost through Adam in Eden, He, as "the second Adam, the Lord from heaven," will restore to us in fuller measure in the paradise of God.

The bondage of sin under which we "groaned, being burdened," He will release us from by breaking the yoke of the oppressor, and letting the oppressed go free.

It must have seemed very strange to the Nazarethites to hear this young man, whom they had known in his obscurity of twenty-five years, apply this grand Messianic prophecy to himself. There must have arisen in their minds a singular commingling of wonder and incredulity, blended perhaps with fear, lest he who had all along been the good and gentle Jesus had lost his mental balance and was going to set up himself as the Messiah.

To understand the feelings they experienced, place yourselves in their situation. What would be your emotions if on some Lord's day, as you sat in your usual seat in the Lord's house, a man of good repute, yet humble parentage, whom you had known from childhood, whom you had seen as a child, as a growing boy, as a working apprentice, as a common mechanic, whose parents you knew, whose home you knew, whom you had met in your daily walks, and who for years had gone with you and sat near you in the house of God, should suddenly, after the lessons for the day had been read which depicted in glowing language the office and work of the Messiah, say, "This day is this scripture fulfilled in your ears"? How such a declaration from such a person would startle you! how almost indignant it would make you! how you would be tempted to sneer and ridicule such claims, or be overwhelmed with alarm at such unrebuked blasphemy! Like the men of Nazareth, you would say, "Is not this the one whom we have known, and whose parents we know, and whose occupation we know? Why, then, speaks he thus? Can he expect us to believe his words? Shall we not rather adjudge him to be insane?"

If you will look at the scene from this point of view, you will more readily comprehend how marvelously astounding this claim of Jesus must have seemed to his fellow-townsmen.

They looked indeed for a Messiah. It was

the one great hope of their nation. It was the burden of their prophecies, the substance of their types, the foreshadowing of their Levitical ritual, the theme of their national psalms, and all their future triumph over their enemies and their exaltation as a nation centred in this long looked-for Messiah. To their blinded minds he was to come in glory and reign with a splendor surpassing that of Solomon. He was to be surrounded with all the insignia of divine royalty. For this "Carpenter," the reputed son of a carpenter, to appropriate to himself these prophetic epithets, and announce that in his person these scriptures found their fulfillment, was indeed too much to be borne, and no wonder, therefore, that they said, "Is not this Joseph's son?"

Perceiving their unbelief and knowing what was in their hearts, Jesus said unto them, "Ye will surely say unto me this proverb, Physician, heal thyself. Whatsoever we have heard done in Capernaum do also here in thy country." Though these were the words of Christ, yet he spoke them as being the sentiments of his hearers, whose thoughts he knew and expressed. It was as if they had said, "We have heard that you have done great works in Capernaum: do them here also, that we may see and judge for ourselves, and not have only the hearsay evidence of public rumor." It was an implied censure on him for working miracles in that almost Gentile town before he wrought any in Nazareth.

To these murmuring thoughts, and perhaps expressions, Jesus replied, "No prophet is accepted in his own country," or, as St. Mark records it, "A prophet is not without honor but in his own country and among his own kin and in his own house."

This proverbial expression finds its truth in that deep-rooted principle of human nature not to give full credit to that, with the gradual growth and unfolding of which we are familiar, and to prefer the foreign and the unknown, over that which originates out of ourselves and is home-born. Minute knowledge of a man's character, and of a man's surroundings, tends, in the minds of those thus familiar, to detract from his greatness. It is so much easier for the human mind to detect flaws, than perceive greatness, so much more ready to note the evil than the good of our fellow-men, so much more inclined to cavil than to praise, that we see every day the truth of the proverb and how peculiarly fitted it was to express just the position in which our Lord, as a Prophet, stood to the querulous and unbelieving Nazarethites.

"But I tell you of a truth," he continues, "many widows were in Israel in the days of Elias, when the heaven was shut up three years and six months, when great famine was throughout all the land, but unto none of them was Elias sent save unto Sarepta, a city of Sidon, unto a woman that was a widow. And many lepers were in Israel in the time of Eliseus the prophet, and none of them was cleansed saving Naaman the Syrian." These instances are quoted by our Lord in order to prove that they who are nearest to the means of grace and opportunities of conviction are often least inclined to profit by them, on which account they are justly granted to others of a more humble and teachable disposition.

It seems, however, greatly to have galled the people, not only that our Lord wrought miracles in Capernaum before he did in Nazareth, but that he should defend his course of conduct by two such anti-Jewish examples of God's dealing with men, whereby a Zidonian woman and a Syrian nobleman—Gentiles—received divine favors denied to the lepers of Judah or the famine-stricken of Israel.

They had implied in their talk with him, "Whatsoever we have heard done in Capernaum do also here in thy country. You wrought miracles there, why not here?" His replying in the way he did was virtually saying to them, "You are unworthy of it, as Israel of old was unworthy of the prophets Elijah and Elisha, who therefore were sent to work miracles among the Gentiles. Elijah was sent to a heathen woman, and a heathen man was sent to Elisha." Thus, not only was their national pride rebuked, but they learned, from these instances of blessings given by some of their greatest prophets to persons outside the pale of Israel, the lesson that the Gentiles were to be called in to participate in the covenant blessing of the God of Abraham.

The people were quick to see and to apply these striking words and facts, and "all they in the synagogue, when they heard these things, were filled with wrath, and rose up and thrust him out of the city, and led him unto the brow of the hill whereon their city was built, that they might cast him down headlong." What a sudden change! Behold the excited throng! The solemn services of the Synagogue are rudely interrupted; the ruler waits not to give the parting blessing; the people tarry not for a benediction, but, "filled with wrath," rise up with tumult and thrust the meek and lowly Jesus out of the house, push him along the narrow streets with noise and insult and violence, and lead him to the steep sides of the mountain which overlooks their town, that from its brow "they might cast him down headlong." Their murderous design was, however, miraculously thwarted, for our Lord, "passing through the midst of them," eluded their grasp, "went his way and came down to Capernaum."

Several places are pointed out as this "brow of the hill." The city is not built on a plain, nor yet on a mountain, but rather on the sides of hills which partially surround it. Up these slopes the town creeps by means of its winding streets and perched houses, while one hill, in particular, overlooks the town very much as the brow does the human face. In our walks around Nazareth we saw one place which remarkably well accords with the description in the text, where, on a rocky wall rising forty or fifty feet, is built the Maronite church, and which the Greeks say is the real spot indicated by St. Luke. This is just on the edge of the city; is on what might fitly be called the "brow of the hill," and overhangs it with sufficient height and perpendicularity to cause the death of any one who should be cast headlong from its top.

According to the Latin or Romish Church, the "Mount of Precipitation" is two miles distant on a peak which does not overlook the city, but overhangs the northern edge of the plain of Esdraelon. To meet the objections made against this place as too remote from Nazareth, the monks reply that old Nazareth once stood there, and that the new Nazareth does not occupy the ancient site. Yet in this so-called new Nazareth (and which is indeed new in all its buildings, not one being here now which was in existence at the time St. Luke wrote) they pretend to show the grotto of the Annunciation, the house of the Virgin, the workshop of Joseph! Their stories, alas! do not agree; they are out of joint, and hence we give them all to the winds as worthless fables, forged by the father of lies to deceive a relic-worshiping world.

Passing from these scenes, let us briefly gather up the lessons which this Sabbath of Jesus at Nazareth teaches.

The first is, that the utmost purity of life and wisdom of speech will not secure its possessor from the assaults of the ungodly. The Nazarethites could not bring against Jesus a single charge affecting his moral character, or a single sound argument to gainsay his gracious words. He was literally "holy, harmless, undefiled, separate from sinners, full of wisdom and of the grace of God." Yet he was hustled out of the Synagogue and thrust along the highway and pressed upon and insulted by the crowd, and led away with murderous purpose as if he had been a thief or a murderer. So that all his past spotless life, his years of acknowledged goodness, were outweighed by the momentary exasperation of a people chafing under the power of truth.

The second lesson shows us the power of prejudice to blind the eye, deafen the ear, shut the heart and warp the judgment against the highest excellence. The prejudice in the case of these people arose from their long-continued familiarity with Jesus. It was an illustration of the old proverb, "Familiarity breeds contempt," and also of our Lord's own remark, "A prophet is not without honor save in his own country." Had they not known him from his youth, had he come to them from afar, had they been unable to say, "Whose father and mother we know, and his brethren and sisters, are they not with us?" he would have met with a different reception. They would not have had these prejudices to hoodwink their eyes and thus prevent their seeing the excellences which shone out from Him against whom their rage was so aroused.

It shows us lastly the unfaltering perseverance of Satan in his attempts to break down Jesus.

He had instigated Herod the king to destroy the infant Jesus, but had been thwarted by the flight into Egypt. He had tried to overthrow his moral and Messianic character and bring him into allegiance to himself by his three temptations in the wilderness. Routed in this conflict by "the sword of the Spirit" as wielded by Jesus, he now employs new measures of assault, and stirs up the jealousy and prejudice of his townspeople as a means of destroying him, making them the instruments of his hate. In this our Lord is an example to all his followers, who must expect and be prepared for all kinds of temptations and assaults from the enemy of their souls, for "the disciple is not above his master, nor the servant above his lord." It is, however, comforting to know that as Christ overcame in every conflict, directly from Satan or indirectly through his emissaries, so we are assured that we shall finally conquer through him, "for in that he himself hath suffered, being tempted, he is able to succor them that are tempted." That succor, given in answer to prayer, will enable us to come off more than conquerors through Christ that loved us.

F

CHAPTER IV.

THE FIRST SABBATH IN CAPERNAUM.

HIS PREACHING.

"And they went into Capernaum; and straightway on the Sabbath day he entered into the Synagogue and taught. And they were astonished at his doctrine, for he taught them as one that had authority, and not as the scribes. And there was in their Synagogue a man with an unclean spirit; and he cried out, saying, Let us alone; what have we to do with thee, thou Jesus of Nazareth? art thou come to destroy us? I know thee who thou art, the Holy One of God. And Jesus rebuked him, saying, Hold thy peace, and come out of him. And when the unclean spirit had torn him, and cried with a loud voice, he came out of him. And they were all amazed, insomuch that they questioned among themselves, saying, What thing is this? what new doctrine is this? for with authority commandeth he even the unclean spirits, and they do obey him. And immediately his fame spread abroad throughout all the region round about Galilee." MARK i. 21-28.

"And came down to Capernaum, a city of Galilee, and taught them on the Sabbath days. And they were astonished at his doctrine, for his word was with power. And in the Synagogue there was a man which had a spirit of an unclean devil, and he cried out with a loud voice, saying, Let us alone; what have we to do with thee, thou Jesus of Nazareth? art thou come to destroy us? I know thee who thou art, the Holy One of God. And Jesus rebuked him, saying, Hold thy peace, and come out of him. And when the devil had thrown him in the midst, he came out of him and hurt him not. And they were all amazed, and spake among themselves, saying, What a word is this! for with authority and power he commandeth the unclean spirits, and they come out. And the fame of him went out into every place of the country round about. LUKE iv. 31-37.

CAPERNAUM AND SEA OF GALILEE.

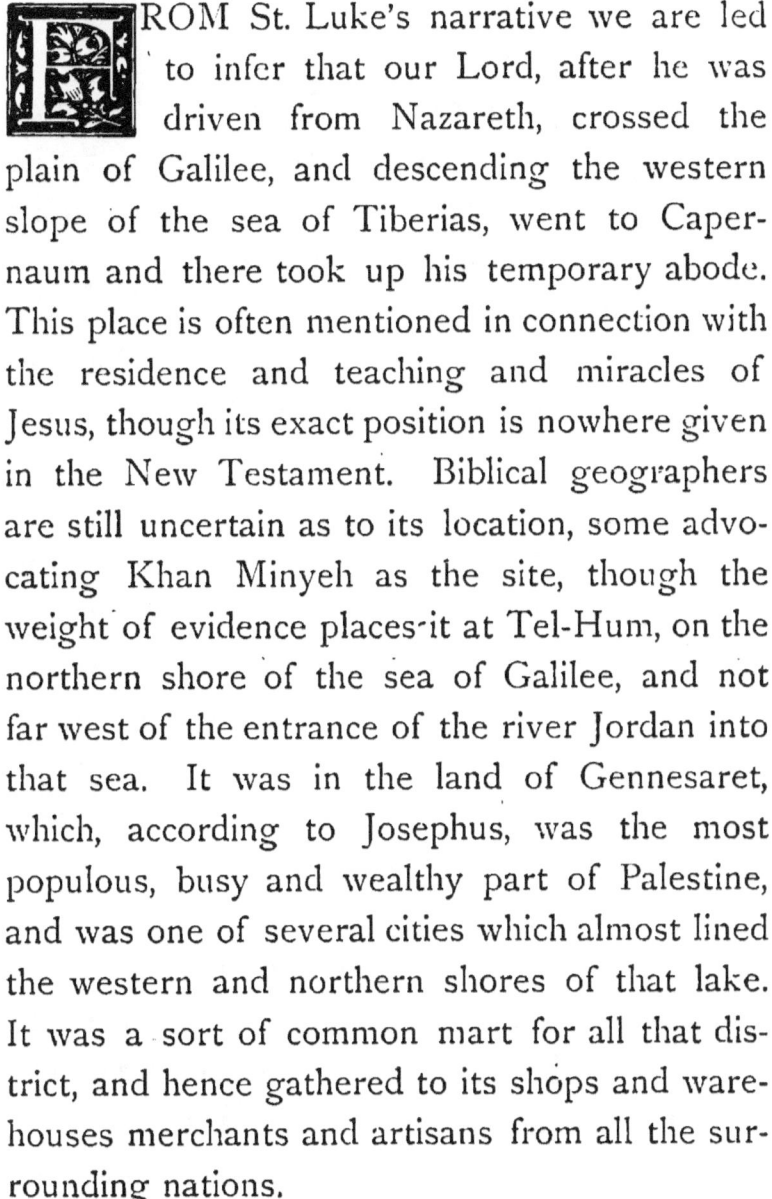ROM St. Luke's narrative we are led to infer that our Lord, after he was driven from Nazareth, crossed the plain of Galilee, and descending the western slope of the sea of Tiberias, went to Capernaum and there took up his temporary abode. This place is often mentioned in connection with the residence and teaching and miracles of Jesus, though its exact position is nowhere given in the New Testament. Biblical geographers are still uncertain as to its location, some advocating Khan Minyeh as the site, though the weight of evidence places it at Tel-Hum, on the northern shore of the sea of Galilee, and not far west of the entrance of the river Jordan into that sea. It was in the land of Gennesaret, which, according to Josephus, was the most populous, busy and wealthy part of Palestine, and was one of several cities which almost lined the western and northern shores of that lake. It was a sort of common mart for all that district, and hence gathered to its shops and warehouses merchants and artisans from all the surrounding nations.

Nothing but a mass of crumbling ruins now exists to mark a spot once the busiest in all northern Palestine. Its glory has departed, and desolation occupies its site.

When our Lord came to Capernaum, he came to a large and flourishing town, which, by its ships and its caravans, had commercial relations with all the region round about; and here he came in contact with the upland farmers, the city mechanics, the lake fishermen, the Gaulonite traders, the merchants from Damascus, the Roman soldiers from Tiberias, the hated publican, the courtly nobleman, the learned scribe, the haughty Pharisee. Jew and Gentile, bond and free, all were found here. It was just the kind of centre, therefore, which Jesus would choose for the better dissemination of his word and works. It was a great distributing point of thought and influence, and hence by putting himself there he was enabled to scatter more widely the seed of the word, and to do more to attract attention and mould the thought of Jew and Gentile than if he had restricted himself to Jerusalem. Jerusalem, the sacred city, the municipal guardian of the Temple, was under the dominion of the Priests, the Pharisees and the Herodians. Against Jesus, as a common enemy, they all combined, and he could not, therefore, with any prospect of success, have established himself there. Their subsequent treatment of him showed what spirit they were of. His aim during his earthly ministry was to get a hearing. His miracles were wrought to attract attention to his words and to certify their divinity. He wanted the people to see his works and hear his words, and nowhere could this so well be accomplished as by taking up a temporary abode in this commercial town, which is accordingly spoken of as " His own city."

St. Mark says, " Straightway on the Sabbath day he entered into the Synagogue and taught." St. Luke says that he came down to Capernaum and "taught them on the Sabbath days"—*i. e.*, on more Sabbaths than one. This was doubtless our Lord's usual Sabbath duty. He had been anointed by the Holy Ghost to preach glad tidings, and he availed himself of the Synagogue to do so week after week while he dwelt in Capernaum. Neither St. Mark nor St. Luke tells us what was the subject-matter of his teaching, but St. Matthew incidentally gives it when (chap. iv. 13), after saying that Jesus, "leaving Nazareth, came and dwelt in Capernaum," and then telling us that this act was a fulfillment of the prophecy of Isaiah in the opening of his ninth chapter, he goes on to state, "From that time (*i. e.*, from the time of his going to Capernaum) Jesus began to preach and to say, Repent, for the kingdom of heaven is at hand." This accords with what St. Mark (i. 14, 15) tells us was the general theme of his discourses in Galilee; viz., "preaching the kingdom of God and saying the time is fulfilled and the kingdom of God is at hand. Repent ye and believe the gospel."

Thus John the Baptist began his ministry as the voice crying in the wilderness, "Repent ye, for the kingdom of heaven is at hand." Thus the apostles began their ministry on the day of Pentecost by preaching the fulfillment of the old prophecies in Jesus of Nazareth, and the necessity of repentance and faith to all who would obtain salvation. The summary of the preaching of Jesus, as recorded by St. Mark, embraces the whole gospel. In declaring that "the time is fulfilled," he claimed that all the Messianic prophecies had culminated in him. In saying that "the kingdom of God," or "of heaven," "is at hand," he plainly showed that his office was that of an inaugurator of this "fifth, universal, heavenly and everlasting kingdom foretold by Daniel (ii. 44; vii. 14, 27), which is to supersede all kingdoms of the earth, and to destroy all that resist it," and that he came to earth, therefore, with the authority of God and the endorsement of Heaven. In calling men "to repent," he announced the initial act which all must do before they can enter into that kingdom, and he clearly declared thereby that an unrepenting and an unbelieving man—*i. e.*, man by nature—man unrenewed by the Holy Ghost —had no place therein; while in requiring all who would become partakers of that heavenly kingdom to "believe the gospel," or the glad tidings which he proclaimed, he taught the absolute necessity of faith as a constant accompaniment of repentance, and as that without which "it is impossible to please God."

Looking at the gospel, as we look at it, through the glass of revelation, and remembering that Jesus regarded it as he and his Apostles have since taught us to regard it, the gospel is but a concrete term for the incarnate Christ. The gospel is "God manifest in the flesh." The gospel is the personal God-man, in whom only is found salvation and eternal life; for Jesus is at once the object of our faith, the fountain of our salvation, the procurer of our pardon, the embodiment of all truth, the one only way to God, the giver of eternal life, the one in whom dwelleth all the fullness of the Godhead bodily. To believe the gospel is, then, to believe in Jesus—to believe in and accept him, in his person, as God manifest in the flesh; in his office, as the Saviour of the world, the anointed Messiah; and in his work as the reconciler of man to God, the destroyer of the works of the devil and the author of eternal salvation.

In what a glorious attitude does this present our dear Lord! An incarnate God! Every gospel blessing, every gospel truth, every gospel grace, every gospel glory, meeting in and dwelling permanently in him, even as all light, all heat, all the elements of beauty, all the constituents of bodily life, dwell in and flow from the central sun. Jesus, in his conscious divinity, knew this, and hence he required all his disciples to believe in him, to honor him, to drink of him as out of a living well-spring, to feed on him as a living bread sent down from heaven, to abide in him as the branch abideth on the vine, and to grow up into him as head over all things to the Church which is his body." Had Plato or Socrates, or any of the great teachers of ancient philosophy, thus spoken, how would they have been derided and come to naught! They told men to believe in certain dogmas elaborated in certain schools, but never did they say to their disciples in the porch, the grove or the academy, Believe in me, "I am the way, the truth, the life. No man cometh unto the Father but by me." This separates Jesus from all other teachers, and this lifts up his truth above all human doctrines, and gives to the humble Preacher in the Synagogue of Capernaum a power and a glory, before which the proudest names of human philosophy fade away as do the stars before the light of a noonday sun.

With reference to the effect of Christ's teaching on the Sabbath in Capernaum two facts are stated.

First, it is said "that they were astonished at his doctrine." This might mean either that the people were astonished that one in such humble life should be able to speak so well and fluently, or else indicates their surprise at the new truths which he proclaimed.

Either of these would constitute a good ground of astonishment to the Capernaumites, for, to all outward appearance, he was but an ordinary workman from despised Nazareth, who neither by birth, social standing nor education had any special claim to their regard.

But much as they were surprised at the force and authority with which he spoke, there is no doubt that the real ground of their astonishment was the astounding truths which he uttered.

These, as we have just seen, though only hinted at by the Evangelist, were yet the great themes of Hebrew prophecy and Hebrew hope for thousands of years, and therefore all true Jewish hearts must have been stirred up by their new proclamation. But then the way in which these Messianic prophecies were fulfilled, and the manner in which the kingdom of the long looked-for Messiah was to be entered and enjoyed, was something entirely different from all their preconceived notions, and offended their pride and all the instincts of the natural heart.

Our Lord, in his several discourses in Capernaum, doubtless went into most interesting unfoldings of type and prophecy and ritual of the Old Testament, and of the Jewish economy. He explained to them the hitherto obscure passages of the Scriptures; he applied to himself their words as they taught the doctrine of the Messiah and his holy and universal reign.

And then, too, he urged them to repentance, to faith or belief in the gospel. He did not urge more frequent attendance at the Synagogue, more frequent sacrifices at the altar, more fastings, more tithings, more pilgrimages to the holy city. He did not flatter their national pride as Jews or foster their false hopes of salvation because they were the children of Abraham. On the contrary, passing by all those things in which the Jews most prided themselves, and by which he might gain for himself personal popularity, he, like John the Baptist, lays the axe at the root of the tree, and declares that entrance into the kingdom of God is not obtained by being a Jew simply, by the sacrifices of the law, by accepting the traditions of their fathers, by any of the works which they do "to be seen of men," by the most rigid Phariseeism or by the most scrupulous Judaism, but only by repentance and faith—a "repentance" which is the result of conscious sin and guilt in the sight of God, which brings to one moral level Jew and Gentile, which respects not words, but the inmost feelings of the soul, which makes one feel his vileness and causes him to cry out for mercy; and a "faith," or belief, in the gospel which enables one to recognize Jesus as the Saviour whom "God hath set forth to be the propitiation for sin," and to accept him as a personal Saviour in all the fullness and freeness of his divine grace. These were new truths to the Capernaumites, and well might they be "astonished" at their bold enunciation, for it is said that "His word was with power."

The second marked effect of his preaching was that they immediately drew a distinction between the teaching of Jesus and that of the scribes: "He taught as one that had authority, and not as the scribes."

This contrast is exceedingly interesting, as it unlocks to us the wretched state of public teaching then common in the Synagogues and schools, and places it in strong opposition to the pure, clear, pungent doctrine of the blessed Jesus.

The scribes were the learned class among the

Jews, and were the recognized custodians and expounders of the law of Moses and of the prophets. They were usually of Priestly or Levitical rank; to them was specially entrusted the multiplication of copies of the Old Testament, to the study of which they devoted themselves with much assiduity. "Our fathers," said Simon the Just, one of their great scribes, 300 years B. C., "have taught us three things—to be cautious in judging, to train many scholars and to set a fence about the law." As transcribers of the law they acquitted themselves with wonderful accuracy and conscientiousness. Nothing could exceed their care of the sacred text. They were scrupulously minute as to words, letters and points. To their minute accuracy and watchful fidelity we owe the preservation of the very words of the Old Testament. They looked with superstitious reverence upon every letter and numeral of the divine word, and guarded it from any admixture of man with jealous care. Yet while thus vigilant as to the letter of Scripture, and while nothing would have induced them to add a "jot" or "tittle" to the text, they virtually made void the law by their traditions. These traditions, or current precepts, which had been handed down to them from their fathers, were concreted into the Mishna. To this code was added the Gemara, in which were gathered the decisions of Rabbis, the fables of Jewish superstition, and together these constituted the Talmud, or the great body of rabbinical law. This work, the Jerusalem Talmud, though not published until the fourth century after Christ, is a transcript, however, of what was held and taught orally in our Lord's day, and enables us to see the puerility, the superstition, the folly, the blasphemy even, of those traditions of the scribes and elders which Jesus so rebuked in his sermon on the mount and in all his interviews with this class. Witness his denunciation of them as recorded in the twenty-third chapter of St. Matthew, where, after saying that "the scribes and Pharisees sit in Moses' seat. All therefore whatsoever they bid you observe, that observe and do," he goes on to say, "But do not ye after their works, for they say and do not, for they bind heavy burdens and grievous to be borne, and lay them on men's shoulders, but they themselves will not move them with one of their fingers; but all their works they do for to be seen of men; they make broad their phylacteries and enlarge the borders of their garments, and love the uppermost rooms at feasts, and the chief seats in the Synagogues, and greetings in the market, and to be called of men, Rabbi, Rabbi." Then, warning his hearers against following them, our Lord utters eight woes against them, which may be considered as eight counts in his indictment against this law-perverting and soul-destroying class. In these denunciations against these hypocrites he thus charges them: "Ye shut up the kingdom against men, for ye neither go in yourselves, neither suffer ye them that are entering to go in." "Ye devour widows' houses, and for a pretence make long prayers." "Ye compass sea and land to make one proselyte, and when he is made ye make him twofold more the child of hell than yourselves." "Ye blind guides which say, Whosoever shall swear by the temple, it is nothing, but whosoever shall swear by the gold of the temple, he is a debtor. Whosoever shall swear by the altar, it is nothing, but whosoever sweareth by the gift that is upon it, he is guilty. Ye pay tithes of mint and anise and cummin, and have omitted the weightier matters of the law, judgment, mercy, faith." "Ye strain at a gnat and swallow a camel." "Ye make clean the outside of the cup and of the platter, but within they are full of extortion and excess." "Ye are like whited sepulchres, which indeed appear beautiful outward, but are within full of dead men's bones and of all uncleanness; even so ye also outwardly appear righteous unto men, but within ye are full of hypocrisy and iniquity." "Ye serpents, ye generation of vipers, how can ye escape the damnation of hell?" This was the deliberate judgment of Him who "knew what was in man," who knew the thoughts and intents of the heart, and whose judgment was just and true. We can scarcely imagine a class of men who, considering their official position, their social standing and their avowed sanctity, were more thoroughly rotten and morally leprous than these blind guides who sat in Moses' seat, and who were the recognized expounders of God's holy law. How great and deep-seated must have been the crimes of these people to call out from the meek and lowly Jesus such maledictions! How he rose above all personal considerations of interest or of fear, when he thus publicly, and renewedly, denounced such woes, not against the lowest orders of society, but against the highest and most learned class, the most powerful in State and Synagogue, the very men whom he knew would in a few days crown their life of infamy by putting him to a death of shame!

Of the puerility of the teachings of these scribes instances might be adduced sufficient to fill a volume; only a few need be inserted here as indicative of all. From the text, "Thou hast fashioned me behind and, before," they deduced the conclusion that Adam was made with two faces, and that Eve was made by sawing him asunder. "If a man should be born with two heads, on which forehead should he bind the phylacteries?" is a sample of the subjects of their most serious discussions. On the feast of Purim the pious Jew was recommended to make himself so mellow that he should not be able to distinguish between "Cursed be Haman" and "Blessed be Mordecai."

From the Mosaic provision of divorce the conclusion was drawn that a man might divorce his wife whenever he found a woman handsomer and more to his liking, since his wife no longer found favor in his eyes. But enough of this. Yet with few exceptions such was the general tone of the teaching in the schools and in the Synagogues, by the scribes and Pharisees, the recognized doctors of the law.

It required, therefore, not much sagacity to discern the difference between our Lord's teaching and theirs, and to contrast the power of the truth and the authority of the speaker with the emptiness of the doctrines and the hesitancy and uncertainty of those who thus taught for commandments the traditions of men.

They were doubtful teachers, not fully believing the truths they pretended to expound. They were false teachers, setting aside the great truths of Jehovah for the puerile comments of men, exalting the ceremonial over the moral law, and making the essence of religion to consist in washing of hands and pots and kettles, in the breadth of the border of the garment, in the size and number of the phylacteries, in the tithing of anise and mint and cummin, rather than in love to God and in a life of obedience to his commandments. This led to the complete ignoring of that grand Messianic scheme which was the central theme of all their law, their prophecy, their ritual, their theocracy, and which, had it been rightly taught, would have fired their hearts, quickened their minds and inspired them with holiest hopes and a living faith.

For this was the "power" that accompanied Jesus' teaching. He taught not the silly sputterings of babbling scribes, but the great utterances of God as comprehended by his divine mind.

He spoke not doubtingly or with uncertainty as to what was or was not right and good and true, as they did, but with the "authority" and the positiveness of incarnate truth, speaking, as he said to Nicodemus, "that we do know, and testifying that we have seen."

Could there be greater contrasts as to the persons who taught, the manner in which they spoke, the doctrines they inculcated, and the effects which followed?

Well might they be "astonished at his doctrine, for his word was with power."

CHAPTER V.

THE FIRST SABBATH IN CAPERNAUM.
(Continued.)

CHRIST'S WORKS IN THE SYNAGOGUE.

WE have seen the "power" of Christ's word on the Sabbath: let us now consider the "power" of Christ's deeds at the same time and place.

The subject thus introduced is that of persons possessed with devils, or demoniacal possession. That there were such cases in our Lord's day is proven by the frequent mention of them in the New Testament. In the Gospels generally, in James ii. 19, and in Rev. xiv. 15 the demons are spoken of as spiritual beings at enmity with God, and having power to afflict man, not only with disease, but, as is marked by the frequent epithet, "unclean," with spiritual pollution also. They "believe" in the existence of Christ, "and tremble." They recognize Jesus as the Son of God, and acknowledge the power of his name used in exorcism by his appointed ministers as equal to the name of Jehovah (Acts xix. 15), and look forward in terror to the judgment to come. The description is precisely that of a nature akin to the angelic in knowledge and power, but with the emphatic addition of the idea of positive and active wickedness. That these evil spirits were permitted by God at that time to possess certain persons does not, in the face of the facts of the New Testament, admit of a doubt. That they are not merely "symbolic utterances," "unreal in actual life," as the mythical school teaches, is evident from the way in which all these narratives are introduced, so that, if they are myths, all else is mythical; they are part and parcel of the same web of history, and are with other facts its warp and woof. Take one set away, and you destroy the whole texture. If these are myths, then all that is miraculous in the Bible is a myth, and Judaism as the conservator of the covenant promises of God, of the truth of God, of the worship of God and the usherer in of the Messiah; and Christianity as the ripe fruit of that budding and blossoming Judaism, with all its grand and elevating influences upon the world of politics, the world of letters, the world of morals, the world of art, are no better than the mythology of Homer or the theogony of Hesiod. That they were not, as some suppose, mere cases of moral insanity, though they have many symptoms in common, is proved by the fact that our Lord addresses himself several times to the demon itself, speaks to him and of him as something distinct from the man himself, as when he said (Mark i. 25), "Hold thy peace and come out of him;" from the fact, that they had a personal knowledge of Christ as being not as the Jews generally called him, "the Son of David," but as "the Son of God;" and again they said, "We know thee who thou art, the holy One of God;" from the fact, that they asked questions aside from anything that could have been personal to the man possessed, and they marked their own individualism and their perfect distinctness of personality from the unfortunates whom they temporarily subjected to their thrall, by asking, "If thou cast us out, suffer us to go away into the herd of swine." These, with many other facts and reasons, abundantly discriminate these cases from those which in our day are classed under the head of moral insanity. That theory completely fails to meet and satisfy all the demands of the various cases stated in the Gospels.

That our Lord fell in with the common belief of the day, and used the superstitious language of the times in order not only not to run counter to the Jewish prejudices, but also and especially thereby to augment the greatness of his pretended cures, is to attribute to him falsehood in speaking what he knew to be untrue; dissimulation in countenancing gross error; and a pandering to the popular taste and sentiment such as can be found in no one act of his whole life.

It would make our blessed Lord deceitful, cringing, hypocritical and false. "The allegiance we owe to Christ as the King of truth, who came not to fall in with men's errors, but to deliver men out of their errors, compels us to believe that he would never have used language which would have upheld and confirmed so serious an error in the minds of men as the belief in satanic influences which did not in truth exist, for this error, if it was an error, was so little an innocuous one, such as might be left to drop naturally away, did, on the contrary, reach so far in its consequences, entwined its roots so deeply among the very ground truths of religion that he would never have suffered it to remain at the hazard of all the misgrowths which it could not fail to occasion."

"Even had not the moral interests at stake been so transcendent, our idea of Christ's absolute veracity, apart from the value of the truth which he communicated, forbids us to suppose that he could have spoken as he did, being perfectly aware all the while that there was no corresponding reality to justify the language which he used. Take, for instance, his words (Luke xi. 17–26. His reply to those who said he cast out devils by Beelzebub the prince of devils), and assume him to have known all the while he was thus speaking that the whole Jewish belief of demoniac possessions was utterly baseless, that Satan exercised no such power over the bodies or spirits of men, that, indeed, properly speaking, there was no Satan at all, and what should we have here for a king of truth?"

It involves more difficulties and requires more credulity to accept the rationalistic and mythical explanations of these passages, than to believe the generally received and literal interpretation of them as declaring "that there are evil spirits, subjects of the evil one, who in the days of the Lord himself, and his Apostles especially, were permitted by God to exercise a direct and controlling influence over the souls and bodies of certain men, producing violent agitations and great sufferings both mental and corporeal."

While we confess, then, that there is much that is mysterious and inexplicable in the several narratives of the demoniacs, we are bound by all the laws of evidence and reason to accept their statements, not only because they are part and parcel of one grand revelation, and so cannot be disjointed and removed without detriment to the whole, but also because they are more easily explained in the position they hold, and by their surroundings in the several Gospels, than by any other system of interpretation.

"For this purpose," says St. John, "the Son of God was manifested, that he might destroy the works of the devil;" and surely by no method could our Lord make this appear more visible or tangible to men, than by healing all manner of diseases which constituted one crop of Satan's sowings in our bodies, and by casting out devils from those, whom the prince of darkness had brought under his thrall; for in both cases there was a direct appeal to men's senses—to their absolute knowledge of things as an evidence of good results effected—which they could not, in the face of the facts, deny.

Let us now consider the miracle itself. In the Capernaum Synagogue, drawn thither by impulses which we cannot know, was one of the demoniacs—one who, as St. Mark says, had "an unclean spirit," or, as St. Luke writes, he "had a spirit of an unclean devil."

The terms "clean" and "unclean" are borrowed from the Levitical law, where certain things, certain acts and certain conditions were termed by that law as being "unclean" or defiling, and as necessarily excluding such persons or things from participation and use in the rites and ceremonies of that ritual. David used the terms to express spiritual purity or holiness. Hence he says, "Create in me, O God, a clean heart." "Cleanse thou me from my secret faults;" and in reply to the question, "Who shall ascend into the hill of the Lord?" the Psalmist replies, "He that hath clean hands and a pure heart," etc.

The gospel use of the term unclean is equivalent to sinful, or unholy, and means the absence of purity, of soundness, of goodness, of holiness.

All sin is uncleanness, and it is thus spoken of in a general term by the apostle when he says, "God hath not called us unto uncleanness, but unto holiness."

Our blessed Lord also, speaking to his disciples, said of them, after he had washed their feet (John xiii. 10, 11), "Ye are clean, but not all, for he knew who should betray him, therefore said he, Ye are not all clean."

The uncleanness of sin results from the fact that it attacks the holiness of God, and would, were it universally prevalent, eradicate all purity from the world. Sin is the work of the devil, for the apostle says (1 John iii. 8), "He that committeth sin is of the devil, for the devil sinneth from the beginning." He is the moral antagonist of Jehovah. He is, therefore, by this very antagonism, unclean, unholy, the opposite of whatever God is in his perfection. There is in him no moral uprightness, no truth, no purity, no goodness. He is "the enemy and the opponent of all righteousness," and all the deeds he has done since his rebellion in heaven, and all the deeds which he has instigated his servants to do on this earth, from the temptation of Eve in the garden of Eden to this hour, have been unclean, a defiling of man made in the image of God, a defiling of God's law, the reflection of the holiness of God; a defiling of the character and work of Jesus, the brightness of the Father's glory and the express image of his person; a defiling of the revealed will of God as holy men wrote it as they were moved by the Holy Ghost; a defiling of the Church of the living God, the mystical body of Christ, by polluting it with heresy and superstition and evil living of its professors. Thus sin, unclean in its nature, its origin, its influence, seeks ever to make unclean what it touches, and gives to each soul that moral defilement, that spiritual pollution, which makes it in the sight of God unclean, and which requires for its cleansing that, and that alone, which can change its character and give it purity—viz., atoning blood; for it is a great and a sublime and a most comforting truth "that the blood of Jesus Christ his Son cleanseth us from all sins."

Every sinner is thus the servant of an "unclean" master. Every sin is an "unclean" act, and a life of sin is a daily adding of uncleanness to uncleanness until both the substance and the surface of the soul, its inward principles and its outward manifestations, are full of pollution, an object of just abhorrence to holy angels and a holy God, who, we are told, cannot look upon sin but with abhorrence. The man thus possessed "with the spirit of an unclean devil" had, it may be, lucid intervals, and in one of these temporary lulls perhaps he went to the Synagogue. During the teaching of Jesus the man began to manifest symptoms of demoniacal possession; and though it does not appear that our Lord had addressed a word to him, yet he cried out with a loud voice, "Let us alone. What have we to do with thee, thou Jesus of Nazareth? art thou come to destroy us? I know thee who thou art, the holy One of God." Such an interruption of the discourse of Jesus must have spread terror in the minds of the congregation, and we may readily imagine the alarm that would be produced by the presence of a demoniac under the active spell and potency of an unclean spirit, not knowing what he might say or what he might do.

To reassure the trembling audience ready to break away from so dreaded a spectacle, to stop the undesired confession and acknowledgment of the evil one, and to manifest his own power over the unseen spirits thus working their foul work through human agencies, our Lord calls out, not to the man, but to the devil within him, "Hold thy peace and come out of him." He thus recognized the presence within the man of a spiritual agent separate and apart from the man, a duality of existence wherein the human was subjected and captive to the demon who inhabited him, the subordination of the whole man to the power of the devil. To the command of Jesus, "Hold thy peace and come out of him," there was an immediate though reluctant obedience. The unclean spirit was not willing to go, and yet go he must, but go he would not until he had done all the hurt which his limited and impotent rage permitted, and hence it is stated by St. Mark that "when he had torn him and cried out with a loud voice, he came out of him," and by St. Luke, "When the devil had thrown him in the midst, he came out of him and hurt him not." These accounts seem to show that as soon as the unclean spirit heard the word of Christ he threw the man into violent convulsions, during the paroxysm of which he was torn with pain and suffering, so that he fell writhing in the midst of the people, and uttering the loud and terrifying, though inarticulate, cry of blended rage on the part of the devil and torture on the part of the demoniac, so that it sounded through the Synagogue like the yell of a defeated yet still defiant spirit, the unclean spirit departed from him. We have at Mark ix. 26 (cf. Luke ix. 42) an analogous case, although there a paroxysm more violent still accompanies the going out of the foul spirit, "for what the devil cannot keep as his own he will, if he can, destroy; even as Pharaoh never treated the children of Israel so ill as then, when they were just escaping from their grasp. Something similar is evermore finding place, and Satan tempts, plagues and buffets none so fiercely as those who are in the act of being delivered from his tyranny for ever." The exclamation of the man, "Let us alone, thou Jesus of Nazareth; art thou come to destroy us? I know thee who thou art, the holy One of God," showed that the evil spirits knew Christ even in his guise of humanity, as if this man had said, "You appear outwardly as only Jesus of Nazareth, but I know thee who thou art, the holy One of God;" and with this confession as to the person of Jesus there was also implied an acknowledgment of his power and authority over them, for the unclean spirit asked, "Art thou come to destroy us?" They knew that it was the work of the Messiah, whose presence under the garb and name of Jesus of Nazareth they recognized, to destroy the work of the devil and to bind hand and foot and cast into outer darkness, where their worm dieth not and the fire is not quenched, all those his enemies, men or devils, who will not submit lovingly to his sceptre and dominion.

This and other similar confessions of the unclean spirits show also that the devils know what is to be their ultimate fate, that they are to be destroyed; not destroyed by annihilation—that is directly contrary to the clear teaching of the Bible—but destroyed in a sense corresponding with the term "second death;" that destruction of all hope, all love, all peace, all joy, all rest, which will be the doom of the wicked, that dying out within them of everything that once was good, that deadness of the soul to all the high and holy bliss of heaven, that entombment of the disembodied spirit in the eternal prison-house of the lost, where the smoke of their torment ascendeth for ever and ever.

In directing the devil who had made this confession concerning Jesus to "hold his peace," or, literally, "be muzzled," Jesus showed that he wanted not his testimony to His divine mission. The truth needed no witness to it from the "father of lies;" nor was Jesus to be bought off from his purpose of dispossessing this poor man by the flattery of the unclean spirit within him, saying that he was the holy One of God, and that he had the power to destroy him.

What Jesus did in this case we find he did also in others, for it is said in another place, "He suffered not the devils to speak, because they knew him," conscious, perhaps, that their attestation might weaken the force of his words, and subject his ministry and his works to the charge of collusion with the spirits whom he thus appeared to cast out. Indeed, we find that this was at length distinctly charged upon him: "He casteth out devils by Beelzebub, the prince of devils;" and on another occasion, after listening to words which because of their spirituality and power they could not comprehend, the people said,

"He hath a devil, and is mad; why hear ye him?"

The credentials which Jesus demanded of these unclean spirits were not confessions as to his person and his power, but obedience to his word. By going out of men at his bidding, they gave a higher proof of Jesus' divinity and character as the Redeemer from sin, than could possibly arise from all the confessions of all fallen angels. By going out at Jesus' bidding they showed to the world that in him lay a higher power—a power they could not resist, a power that only temporarily held back their foretold destruction—that they and their master and the whole realm of evil which they represented were subordinated to the word of Jesus, and thus acknowledged his superiority.

And when we ponder on it for a moment, what a wonderful testimony to Christ was thus borne to his Messiahship, by the fact that in every instance mentioned in the Gospels, the devils *knew* him, *feared* him, *obeyed* him, *fled* from his presence, and *deprecated his power!* How it tells of the inherent divinity that was thus temporarily overshadowed by his humanity which could speak with such authority! How it tells of his supreme dominion over the whole world of spirits, the good and the bad being alike subjects of his universal rule—the angels to minister unto him, the devils to believe and tremble, both to bow before him!

The effects of this act of Jesus produced great amazement and great questionings. As this was doubtless the first time that he had wrought such a miracle, and the first time that any such dispossession of evil spirits had taken place, they were entirely unprepared for such a manifestation of divine power, such a grappling with the spirits of evil, such an assertion of control over the unseen world, such a concentrating of power in speech, as they then saw in their Synagogue. No wonder they were amazed, confounded, alarmed. No wonder that they questioned with themselves, What a word is this? what new doctrine is this? what thing is this? for with authority and power he commandeth the unclean spirits and they do obey him.

Thus wondering and discussing among themselves at what they had seen and heard, the congregation of the Synagogue broke up into little knots of eager talkers and listeners, and as they went their several ways, they told all they met of what had been done, until the city was rife with the story, and all Capernaum heard with astonishment that the new citizen, Jesus, who had so recently come to their town from Nazareth, had that day spoken words such as their ears never before heard—words of truth and holiness and power—and done a deed that day such as had never been wrought in all Israel, the tangible and living evidence of which was before them in the dispossessed man and the hundred witnessing people, so that they could not gainsay or disbelieve without distrusting the evidence of their senses and the credibility of their friends. This miracle and this teaching gave to Jesus a prominence which drew to him all eyes, all ears, as a great wonder-worker in Israel, for "his fame spread abroad throughout all the region round about Galilee."

CHAPTER VI.

THE FIRST SABBATH IN CAPERNAUM.
(CONTINUED.)

CHRIST OUTSIDE THE SYNAGOGUE.

"And when Jesus was come into Peter's house, he saw his wife's mother laid and sick of a fever. And he touched her hand, and the fever left her, and she arose and ministered unto them. When the even was come, they brought unto him many that were possessed with devils, and he cast out the spirits with his word, and healed all that were sick: that it might be fulfilled which was spoken by Esaias the prophet, saying, Himself took our infirmities and bare our sicknesses." MATT. viii. 14-17.

"And forthwith, when they were come out of the Synagogue, they entered into the house of Simon and Andrew, with James and John. But Simon's wife's mother lay sick of a fever; and anon they tell him of her. And he came and took her by the hand, and lifted her up, and immediately the fever left her, and she ministered unto them. And at even, when the sun did set, they brought unto him all that were diseased, and them that were possessed with devils. And all the city was gathered together at the door. And he healed many that were sick of divers diseases, and cast out many devils, and suffered not the devils to speak, because they knew him." MARK i. 29-34.

"And he arose out of the Synagogue and entered into Simon's house. And Simon's wife's mother was taken with a great fever, and they besought him for her. And he stood over her and rebuked the fever, and it left her, and immediately she arose and ministered unto them. Now, when the sun was setting, all they that had any sick with divers diseases brought them unto him, and he laid his hands on every one of them and healed them. And devils also came out of many, crying out and saying, Thou art Christ the Son of God. And he, rebuking them, suffered them not to speak, for they knew that he was Christ." LUKE iv. 38-41.

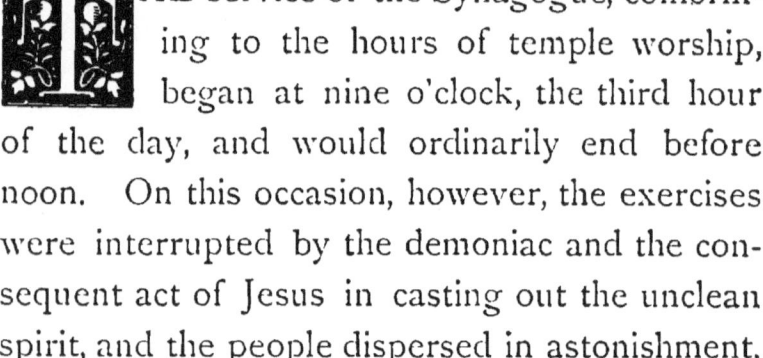HE service of the Synagogue, conforming to the hours of temple worship, began at nine o'clock, the third hour of the day, and would ordinarily end before noon. On this occasion, however, the exercises were interrupted by the demoniac and the consequent act of Jesus in casting out the unclean spirit, and the people dispersed in astonishment, without waiting for the usual benediction.

Jesus had already called Peter and Andrew, James and John, the two pairs of brothers, from their fishing boats and nets to be his disciples and to become "fishers of men," and now, accepting an invitation from the two elder brethren, he goes to the house of Simon Peter for the Sabbath meal, which, according to Josephus, was usually eaten at the sixth hour, or twelve o'clock. The dwelling which he entered is called by St. Matthew "the house of Peter," by St. Mark, "the house of Simon and Andrew," and by St. Luke, "the house of Simon." The two latter evangelists speak of Peter (*i.e.*, rock), surnamed thus by our Lord after his memorable confession of him as "the Christ," by his earlier Syriac name of Simon (*i.e.*, hearer).

St. Mark, who wrote under the special direction of St. Peter, and who, therefore, in the facts concerning him, wrote with greater minuteness of detail, says that the building was "the house of Simon and Andrew," as if it was the joint property of the sons of Jonas, or at least occupied by the families of each.

Here, then, was the home of the two first-called apostles. There is nothing to indicate whether it was large or small, well or poorly furnished, in a prominent or a retired part of the town. All that we know with certainty of their worldly condition is that they were fishermen, that they owned one of the fleet of fishing-smacks, or small vessels, which sailed on the lake, that they owned a dwelling in Capernaum, that Peter was a married man, that Peter's wife's mother was living with them, that they extended their plain hospitality to Jesus by asking him to take his mid-day Sabbath meal with them, that they included James and John in this invitation, and that our Lord rewarded their hospitality by a miracle of mercy to the sick mother-in-law of Peter.

We infer from St. Mark's record that Jesus was not informed of the sickness of Peter's wife's mother until after he had gone to the house, for he says, "He entered into the house of Simon and Andrew, ... and anon they tell him of her." She was "laid," or prostrate, thrown down, on a bed, "sick of a great fever." From the term translated "great," by which St. Luke, himself a physician, characterizes this fever, following therein the distinction made by Galen and the Greek physicians of "great" and "small" fevers, we infer that the sickness was a high grade of Syrian fever, such as is often met with at this day in those regions, and which was frequently and rapidly fatal. No sooner is he informed of her illness than he goes to her room, and standing by her bed, takes her hand, rebukes the fever, gently lifts her up (for all these acts are hinted at by the several writers), and immediately the fever left her and she arises well and strong. The healing medicine here was Christ's rebuking word to the fever. This word "rebuked" is surely worthy of special notice here, for it implies the presence of some hostile power and the rebuking or turning back that power by a superior and controlling power.

The word is the same as that used in quelling the storm upon the Sea of Galilee, when it is said, "Then he arose and rebuked the wind and the sea, and there was a great calm." In the case of the stormy sea there was a great tempest above, together with the raging of the water dashing over the ship, and the rebuke was couched in the words, "Peace, be still." The immediate subsidence of winds and waves into "a great calm" showed how obedient these powers of nature, even in their wildest and most furious state, are to their Lord and Master, and how he makes them, as servitors of his will, do his bidding and submit to his sway. Just so with one tempest-tossed with a raging fever, restless, delirious, so that the whole surface of his being is furrowed with the waves of pain as, like successive billows, they roll over the system in the exacerbations of fever. The rebuke of Jesus to the assailing fever, this boisterous and disturbing power, "Peace, be still," hushes at once its violence, breaks at once its force, drives away at once its pain, restores at once the poised mind, the steady will, the strong limbs, the quiet heart.

The results of this beneficent act of Jesus were immediate: "the fever left her." But it did not leave her, as fevers ordinarily do, with an exhausting weakness after the artificial strength of the febrile attack. It did not leave her prostrated in the contest, requiring care, nursing, food, in order to build up the system and repair the wasted strength through the usual process of slow convalescence, for we are told that not only did the fever leave her, but "she arose and ministered unto them." She proved the soundness and the quickness of her recovery by at once doing the personal services which the rites of hospitality required. Thus the word of Christ not only rebuked the fever, but invoked health, not only banished pain and suffering and weakness, but infused strength, activity and all matronly energy. It was a double miracle. Jesus had, perhaps, never been under that roof before, yet what a blessing he brought to that house! and how the miracle-healed mother must have rejoiced that her son-in-law was the professed disciple of Him who could command not only the wind and the waves, but diseases and devils, and they obey him!

This narrative is also interesting as it incidentally brings out two facts: first, that the apostle Peter was a married man. It was his "wife's mother" that was healed. If Peter, the head of the college of the apostles, the "Rock" on which, as so many contend, the Lord builded his Church, the "founder," as is claimed by self-styled infallibilists, of "the Church of Rome," from whom the pope derives his power of the keys, and up to whom he traces his ecclesiastical lineage,—if Peter could be married, and, as St. Paul says (1 Cor. ix. 5), "Lead about a wife," surely his successors may do the same, for they are not more pure and holy than he, and to forbid any to do it, is to forbid what our Lord himself countenanced and approved. The second fact is, that by his presence in that house, and by his miracle wrought there under those circumstances, he evinced his approval of the marital state in which he found his servant Peter. If Jesus had disapproved of marriage and of marriage feasts, would he have wrought his "beginning of miracles" to enhance the pleasure of a bridal banquet? and if Jesus had disapproved of his ministers having wives and desired them to be celibates, would he have accepted the hospitality of a married apostle and wrought a miracle to heal his wife's mother? Most certainly not.

But the work of the day is not yet over. The Jewish style of reckoning was from sunset to sunset, hence the Sabbath ended with the going down of the sun. The strictness which till that hour had been so scrupulously observed was then relaxed, and works might be done then which it would have been unlawful to do an hour before. But though the solemn observances of the day were over, yet the sacred influence of the Sabbath still lingered, as did the twilight of the Sabbath sun, and while strictness was relaxed, hallowed feelings and words still lingered above the horizon which had hid the setting Sabbath. So soon, therefore, as this hour arrived, we find that all Capernaum is astir. The streets are being filled, and the throngs are directing their steps toward Peter's house. But what a strange motley of people! Not only the usual elements of a crowd, the young and old, man and woman, the higher and the lower classes, the rude and the refined, but see! there is one mother carrying in her arms a sick infant, there is a person leading a blind man, there is a litter borne by two persons on which lies a patient deathly sick, there is a group struggling to get along with them a raving maniac, there is a helpless paralytic carried by his friends, there goes the cripple slowly crawling over the rough pavement. What a strange congregation of sick and diseased and maimed and deaf and dumb and blind and epileptic and demonized persons, yet all eager, all anxious, all with faces set toward one spot! What means this unusual sight, never before seen in that city? Why this gathering to the house of this fisherman? It is because Jesus is there. They have heard of his morning miracle, they have caught rumors of other wondrous works, they recognize among them the presence of One who can do what human love and tenderness, human physicians and surgeons, cannot do, and they come in crowds, some to ask his help for themselves and friends, and others prompted by curiosity to see whether or no this Jesus of Nazareth can do what report says he has done in other places; and so it came to pass, as St. Mark has it, "All the city was gathered together at the door."

Nor were they gathered in vain. The Lord Jesus goes out to them as they crowd the streets and open spaces, and passing from one to another, lays his hands on every one—not one overlooked—and heals them all. He also cast out many devils "with his word," who, as they came out of their victims, cried out, saying,

"Thou art Christ, the Son of God; but Jesus rebuked them and suffered them not to speak, for they knew that he was Christ;" and he was not willing that their impure tongues should proclaim his holy mission, lest, in the perverted minds of those who were ever seeking occasion to denounce him, the testimony of these unclean spirits to his person and mission might mar the work which he came to accomplish.

What a Sabbath evening scene was that! As one after another was healed and stood up in the full flush of health, as the cripple walked, as the blind saw, as the dumb spake, as the crooked was made straight, as the paralytic became strong, as the sick were made well, how each in turn must have added to the common stock of joy, each caused fresh wonder to the gaping crowd, each observed the exhaustless fullness of healing grace which showed itself as strong in casting out the last devil as in curing the first fever! The shadows of the evening crept over the surrounding hills, the short but lovely twilight had departed, and the stars looked down and glassed themselves in the mirror-like lake below them, before the loving work of Jesus was over, and there remained not a sick or demoniac person in that whole city of Capernaum except such as may have refused to go to Jesus. Who can tell the joy that Jesus thus sent into many hearts and many homes? Who can measure the sorrow and the suffering which thus, at a word, he drove away? and as the citizens after such intense excitement settled themselves to their nightly sleep, they must have wondered at the marvelous change which one short hour had wrought in their social life, leaving not a sick person to be watched over or cared for, but all, without exception, could lie down in health and sleep in peace, because the great Healer had scattered broadcast his blessings and taken away the long-existing evils, and given freely, without money and without price, life, health and soundness of mind and body to all who sought his healing power.

St. Matthew gives the keynote to this whole transaction when he adds to his account of it these remarkable words: "That it might be fulfilled which was spoken by Esaias the prophet, saying, Himself took our infirmities and bare our sicknesses." The words of Isaiah (liii. 4), in our English version, are, "Surely he hath borne our griefs and carried our sorrows." The chapter in which these words occur is one of the most touchingly Messianic of all his prophecies.

From the beginning to the end the one theme is the Messiah—Messiah rejected, Messiah suffering, Messiah in his vicarious redemption, Messiah the sin-bearer, Messiah conquering and Messiah in final triumph.

The words, as originally uttered, evidently had a double meaning, referring primarily to Christ's bearing away or carrying away our sins, an act typified by the scapegoat on the great day of atonement, when the selected victim, having had, as it were, laid upon his head by the imposition of the high priest's hands "all the sins of the children of Israel" which they had before confessed, was given over to the hand of a special messenger to be led away into the wilderness, "into a land not inhabited," and was there let loose. Thus symbolically the scapegoat bore away the sins of the people. All this was a figure of Christ, the true sin-bearer, to whom all the types of the Levitical ritual pointed, and who alone "bore away" our sins.

Isaiah uses the words, "griefs," "sorrows," putting the effect for the cause. Sin always, however sweet at the first taste, brings eventual grief and sorrow, and the root of every grief and sorrow that afflicts man is sin. St. Matthew applies it to another form of sin's doings, and still, like Isaiah, putting the effect for the cause, says, after the wondrous putting forth of healing power on that Sabbath evening, "Himself took our infirmities and bare our sicknesses." Sin brings in infirmities and sickness. There is not a cause of human suffering that does not find its origin in sin, and it is the manifold and wide-branching results of sin which cover the earth as with sackcloth, which fill it with sick bodies and diseased souls, which make it a vast lazar-house of infirmity and woe. It is all sin's work, its fruit, its wages.

The taking away of these physical effects of sin—an act beyond all human power—proved that he could take away sin itself, the parent of this progeny of disease and death.

Our Lord himself appeals to this in the case of the man sick of the palsy, for when the scribes objected to his saying to the paralytic, "Thy sins be forgiven thee," charging him with speaking blasphemies and declaring that God only can forgive sin, Jesus simply adds, "But that ye may know that the Son of man hath power on earth to forgive sin, he saith to the sick of the palsy, I say unto thee, arise and take up thy bed, and go thy way into thine house." As if he had said, You challenge my right to forgive sin, you accuse me of blasphemy in saying what I did, because it is the sole prerogative of God to forgive sin. I will, therefore, prove to you that I have the power to forgive sins, and that I am not, as you think, a blasphemer, by giving immediate cure to this paralytic confessedly beyond the reach of all human skill, and the immediate response to the word of Jesus by the paralytic, now no longer crippled with palsy, but suddenly starting up into full health, was the divine attestation and credential of his power to forgive sin.

In a secondary sense, therefore, when Jesus took away the resulting evils of sin, he did fulfill a prophecy which foretold that he should "bear our griefs and carry our sorrows," so that St. Matthew might in truth say, "Himself took our infirmities and bare our sicknesses."

There is no doubt that the healing power which our Lord exercised in and around Peter's house was also accompanied with deep personal consciousness of the evil of sin as thus working out these sad results, and with intense compassion for those afflicted with the grievous maladies. These two feelings, a consciousness of the full evil of sin and a true sympathy with the sufferer from sin, blended in one strong emotion, must have weighed heavily upon the tender and holy heart of Jesus, and burdened his spirit with a grief too deep for human comprehension. It was not with him a cold, mechanical bestowal of healing power, in the giving out of which he was an impassive agent. He did not regard himself as a walking battery of vital forces, needing only a physical, tactual application, to receive the energizing and health-begetting influence, but in all his acts and works we everywhere discover that he weeps with those who weep, mourns with those who mourn, rejoices with those who rejoice, brings his heart in living contact with other hearts, and touches all the faculties and affections of the soul by the manifestations of his sympathetic spirit.

"He realized, as no one else ever did, the law of all true helping, namely, that the burden which you would lift you must yourself stoop to and come under (Gal. vi. 2), the grief which you would console you must yourself feel with; a law which we witness to as often as we use the words "sympathy" and "compassion" was truest of all in him upon whom the help of all was laid. Not in this single aspect of his life alone were these words of the prophet fulfilled, but rather in the life itself, which brought him in contact with the thousand forms of want and woe, of discord in man's outer life, of discord in man's inner being. Every one of these, as a real consequence of sin, and at every moment contemplated by him as such, pressed with a living pang into the holy soul of our Lord. "He could therefore heal neither bodily nor spiritual disease without a deep consciousness of his special relation to man as the Substitute, the Redeemer, the Lamb of God, who was to bear the penalty of the world's guilt. And it is not, we believe, too much to suppose that by a superhuman and perfect compassion he took into his own holy consciousness and truly realized the bodily as well as the spiritual suffering which he removed from others."

What an ennobling idea does this give us of the height and depth and length and breadth of our Lord's compassion! How beautifully does it interpret those heart-soothing words, "We have not a high priest which cannot be touched with the feeling of our infirmities, but was in all points tempted like as we are, yet without sin," and those other words, "For verily he took not on him the nature of angels, but he took on him the seed of Abraham. Wherefore in all things it behooved him to be made like unto his brethren, that he might be a merciful and faithful high priest in things pertaining to God. For in that he himself hath suffered, being tempted, he is able to succor them that are tempted."

> "When gathering clouds around I view,
> And days are dark and friends are few,
> On Him I lean who not in vain
> Experienced every human pain;
> He feels my griefs, he sees my fears,
> And counts and treasures up my tears."

Such is the record of the first Sabbath of our Lord at Capernaum, full of holy words, whose power thrilled hundreds of hearts; full of holy deeds, whose healing effects reached hundreds of the sick and the possessed of devils; and the personal presence of Jesus speaking these holy words, and doing these wondrous deeds, and diffusing these marvelous blessings, made that Sabbath the most noted day ever known in the history of that city.

CHAPTER VI.

THE SABBATH AT THE POOL OF BETHESDA.

"After this there was a feast of the Jews; and Jesus went up to Jerusalem. Now there is at Jerusalem by the sheep market a pool, which is called in the Hebrew tongue Bethesda, having five porches. In these lay a great multitude of impotent folk, of blind, halt, withered, waiting for the moving of the water. For an angel went down at a certain season into the pool, and troubled the water: whosoever then first after the troubling of the water stepped in was made whole of whatsoever disease he had. And a certain man was there, which had an infirmity thirty and eight years. When Jesus saw him lie, and knew that he had been now a long time in that case, he saith unto him, Wilt thou be made whole? The impotent man answered him, Sir, I have no man, when the water is troubled, to put me into the pool: but while I am coming, another steppeth down before me. Jesus saith unto him, Rise, take up thy bed, and walk. And immediately the man was made whole, and took up his bed, and walked: and on the same day was the sabbath. The Jews therefore said unto him that was cured, It is the sabbath day: it is not lawful for thee to carry thy bed. He answered them, He that made me whole, the same said unto me, Take up thy bed, and walk. Then asked they him, What man is that which said unto thee, Take up thy bed, and walk? And he that was healed wist not who it was: for Jesus had conveyed himself away, a multitude being in that place." JOHN v. 1-13.

IN reference to the opening verse of this chapter, Chrysostom says, "Jesus went up to the feast at Jerusalem to show his reverence for the law of Moses, and in

order to preach to the multitudes then assembled there." Certainly he never lost an opportunity of "preaching the kingdom of God," and ever availed himself of casual events and wayside scenes to do good to the souls and to the bodies of men. This is illustrated by his Sabbath work at the pool of Bethesda. This pool or reservoir was situated near St. Stephen's gate—the old sheep-gate—and just outside of the northern wall of the Haram Area. There was evidently a spring or fountain here, which for sanitary purposes had been converted into a large tank by excavating and building around it with solid masonry, so as to hold a large supply of water. On the border of this pool were erected colonnades or porches, consisting of several archways or cloisters, for the use and enjoyment of those frequenting that attractive spot.

It seems that the popular opinion was, as the legend recorded in the fourth verse shows, that at a certain season an angel troubled the water, and then whosoever first stepped in afterward was healed of whatsoever disease he had. This pool was resorted to, therefore, by multitudes of impotent folk, of blind, halt, withered, "waiting for the moving of the waters." That this was the common belief among the Jews cannot be denied. What grounds there were for it we do not know, though the legend must have had some basis or root out of which the widespread superstition as to the angelic troubling and healing grew.

There is some doubt as to the authenticity of this fourth verse, founded on the fact that the words are not found in some very old and important manuscripts and versions, and hence by those who reject the verse it is supposed to be the interpolation of a transcriber, who incorporated into the sacred text what was originally only a marginal gloss of a commentator explaining the healing virtue of the water by stating the current legend of the troubling of it by the angel who periodically bathed in its waters.

Though the absence of this verse from some first-class manuscripts, Uncial as well as Cursive, casts some suspicion on its genuineness, yet there is great weight of evidence on the other side, and the words are found in copies of the gospel in the time of Tertullian, and are quoted as canonical Scripture by some of the earliest and most cautious of the Christian Fathers. The presence or absence of this verse, however, has little to do with the narrative of the miracle, as it only accounts for the poor infirm man being where he was and for so long a time. The miracle which our Lord wrought rests not upon that verse, and hence its omission or retention does not affect the divine transaction.

The traditional pool of Bethesda, called the *Birket Israil*, is now in ruins. Its once capacious basin is nearly filled with rubbish, its once populous colonnades are now fallen, and only two so-called porches or arched recesses are visible. But its locality, its proportions, its surroundings, seem to indicate that that, and not, as some suppose, the Fountain of the Virgin, outside of the gate, in the valley of the Kedron, is the real pool of Bethesda by the sheep-gate or market mentioned by St. John.

The objection made by some to the statement that only one person was healed after each troubling of the water does not necessarily militate with the reception of the verse, because it does not say how often that "certain season" was at which the angel went down into the pool, and it may have been once a month, or once a week, or at irregular but yet numerous times, so that during the year a score or more persons might have been thus healed. Besides, is not the fact as it is recorded, like many other of God's providential dealings with his people? Had not our Lord a little while before, in his discourse in the Synagogue at Nazareth, mentioned two almost analogous cases of God's sovereignty in the disposition of his gifts of grace and healing? "Many widows were in Israel in the days of Elias, when the heaven was shut up three years and six months, when great famine was throughout all the land; but unto none of them was Elias (Elijah) sent save unto Sarepta, a city of Sidon, unto a woman that was a widow. And many lepers were in Israel in the time of Eliseus (Elisha) the prophet, and none of them was cleansed saving Naaman the Syrian." God thus gives or withholds at his pleasure, with or without human or angelic instrumentalities, and none can say, What doest thou? or question his right to do what he will with his own gifts of healing or of grace; and our Lord himself, be it remembered, only healed one of all the multitudes which lay there. Besides, this was a period in the Jewish history when angelic interpositions and miracles were looked for, and did actually occur; and by them, infrequent as they were, the minds of the people were made conversant with them, were prepared to receive them, and the more readily accredited the truths or facts they were designed to herald or attest.

The attempt of some commentators to take the healing efficacy of the waters out of the category of miracles, and attribute it to mere medicinal qualities in the spring, such as are found in the chalybeate or sulphur or other mineral springs in our day, not only conflicts with the words of the text, but suggests the unanswerable questions, If the healing virtue lay in the medicinal character of the water, why were not *all* who stepped into it healed? Why was it restorative only at certain seasons? Why exhaust its efficacy on one case?

Let us now look at the scene which presented itself to our Lord on that Sabbath morning. On his way to the temple he had to pass Bethesda. In its many porches he saw "a great multitude of impotent folk, of blind, halt, withered, waiting for the moving of the water."

There were no hospitals then where the sons and daughters of sickness could be housed and cared for. Those who had money or friends might receive due attention, but the poor and the friendless crawled into the streets or open places of the city, or lay along the highway, objects of pity and compassion, begging alms, imploring relief, exhibiting their sores and deformities, and indebted to the passing stranger for the daily sustenance of a wretched, homeless life. We see much of this at the present time in the East. It is a calamity to be sick anywhere—to be blind or halt under any the most favorable circumstances; but to be diseased and have no hand of friendship to mitigate your suffering, to be blind or deaf or dumb or paralytic and have no commiseration of kindly companionship, to be left all broken down in body and mind to grope along life's pathway halting, stumbling, suffering, dying, with no word of comfort and no arm of succor,—oh, this is wretchedness indeed! This the climax of sorrow! Christ's conduct toward the sick and the afflicted has given birth to all the hospitals and asylums and benevolent institutions of the world. They are the outgrowth of the words and the deeds of Jesus. But for them the world would be now what it was before the advent of Christ, without a hospital or an asylum or a reformatory or any association banded together to dispense relief or comfort to the needy and the disconsolate.

The world owes all the brightness of its benevolence and the glory of its great eleemosynary institutions, and the lofty compassion that rules the minds of thousands, and the grand philanthropy that sees in every human face "a brother," and in every wayside sick man a "neighbor," to the Lord Jesus Christ.

All this is his work—a work, too, incidental to his higher work, though necessarily flowing out of that, for, as that love which brought him to earth to be man's redeemer was infinite, so its overflowings to the sinful and unworthy, even to those who will not receive his offered salvation, are fraught with copious blessings, diffusing their virtue through that network of Christian benevolence which now spreads its meshes over all classes and conditions and makes all whom it can reach the objects of its benedictions.

The sight of so much misery as grouped itself within the porches of Bethesda excites our

Lord's compassion, and he pauses to look upon the heart-sickening scene. Conversing, perhaps, with one and another, he finds a poor cripple who "had an infirmity thirty and eight years," one who in answer to our Lord's question, "Wilt thou be made whole?" told Jesus, "Sir, I have no man when the water is troubled to put me into the pool, but while I am coming another steppeth down before me." The question which our Lord asked of this man, "Wilt thou be made whole?" was put, not because he did not know the desires of this man, but in order, doubtless, to draw the attention of the man to himself as one unusually interested in his case, and also to rouse up perhaps the almost extinct hopes of the man, in whom, after thirty and eight years of suffering, there remained but little anticipation of effectual relief. He wanted to concentrate the man's thoughts and looks upon himself as preliminary to the putting forth of divine healing, just as he asked the blind man, on another occasion, "What will ye that I shall do unto you?" There must be a felt need of outward help on the part of the recipient of Christ's favor, so as to make the favor received recognized as a divine interposition. When

Jesus had brought this infirm man to this state of conscious need and expectance of some kind of blessing (for he must have read the premonition of it in Jesus' benevolent face and kindly words), he said to him, "Rise, take up thy bed, and walk." Instead of stopping to say, "Sir, have I not just told thee that I cannot rise, that if moved at all it must be by the help of others, and that this is the very reason why I cannot avail myself of the troubled waters?" as he might have done, he makes the effort to obey the divine mandate "Rise," and in the effort finds the strength, waiting not until it consciously comes before he puts it forth, but in the act of obedience, finds the power to obey. And so the poor impotent cripple, who had not walked perhaps for thirty-eight years, who was so utterly poor and helpless that he could not command the services of a man to put him into the pool, and who was thus perhaps rendered as hopeless as he was helpless, now stands erect, to the wonder of all around him. He took up the pallet, or rug, on which he had been so long lying, and walked forth in perfect soundness of health and limbs. The change was immediate. It was not the current of returning strength flowing first into one member of the body and giving motion to that, and then into another, swelling out its long-withered muscles, but it was an instantaneous change, bringing with it the full and complete restoration of every physical power to that emaciated, shriveled, weakened, crippled, helpless body. One moment an object of intense pity by reason of his intensified infirmity, the next standing up stalwart and strong in all the freshness and fullness of rejuvenated life!

One would have thought that such a marked manifestation of divine power would have called forth admiration at the deed of Jesus, and that he would have been praised for his abounding mercy. But whatever may have been its effect on some, on others it had the effect of arousing opposition; and unable to find fault with Jesus for speaking a healing word, they turned upon the healed man and accused him of breaking the Sabbath because, at the command of Christ, "he took up his bed and walked." The wonder at the miracle is lost in the pharisaic hypocrisy of zeal for the Sabbath, and hence the Jews said unto him that was cured, "It is the Sabbath day: it is not lawful for thee to carry thy bed."

According to the strict construction of the fourth commandment, and according to the directions of Nehemiah (xiii. 19) and Jeremiah (xvii. 21, et seq.), "to bear no burden on the Sabbath day," it was true that the man was breaking the Sabbath by carrying a "burden," even his bed, on that day. But this declaration of these Sanhedrists, or persons connected with the supreme council of the Jews (for it is to these that St. John refers when he uses the term "Jews"), is a very narrow and carping view to take of that commandment. It was evidently a cover under which to attack Jesus himself, as it subsequently comes out in the sixteenth verse, where the apostle says, "Therefore did the Jews persecute Jesus, and sought to slay him, because he had done these things on the Sabbath day." How intense must their bigotry have been, when it made them blind to the wondrous miracle and keen-sighted as to a supposed breaking of the traditions of their fathers! failing to recognize the blessing vouchsafed in the desire to find fault with the gracious Giver.

The reply of the healed man is at once simple and conclusive: "He that made me whole, the same said unto me, Take up thy bed, and walk." In his mind, evidently, the authority which could work the cure was quite sufficient authority for his carrying his bed. Foiled here, they turn upon the man again and ask, "What man is that which said unto thee take up thy bed, and walk?" The animosity of the Jews leaks out here in the suppression of all allusion to the work of mercy, and in dwelling only on the declared infraction of the law. They ask, not, "What man is that which made thee whole that we may see and admire so gracious a being?" Oh no! they doubtless knew very well who it was, and were only concerned to fix on Jesus the charge of breaking the Sabbath. It seems not a little remarkable, on first thought, that the once impotent man did not know who had healed him. One would have supposed that receiving so great a boon he would at least have inquired the name of the giver, but in the flush and excitement of his cure, the sudden influx into his almost hopeless mind of so unexpected a blessing, he forgot, as it were, all the proprieties of gratitude, and he was more anxious to realize his new-found strength by at once doing what he was told, take up his bed and walk, than to delay for the purpose of ascertaining who was his benefactor. The man was evidently bewildered by the tumultuous emotions which then filled his mind, as we can easily imagine what a whirl there would be in our feelings under similar circumstances. It must be remembered, also, that before the man could recover from his astonishment and collect his thoughts, "Jesus had conveyed himself away, a multitude being in that place." The working of a miracle in so public a spot necessarily drew a large crowd together, and Jesus, unwilling to remain in their midst, glided away, availing himself of the excitement to pass quickly through the multitude, and went onward to the house of God. Thus he did not stop long enough to let the healed man show his gratitude or learn his true character.

Afterward the two, the Healer and the healed, stand together again. They are in the temple. The Healer on his mission of grace, the healed, doubtless, to give thanks for his cure. But the latter does not recognize the former, and not until Jesus speaks to him does he ascertain who it was that had healed him.

The purpose of Jesus in finding him in the

temple was to let the man know his benefactor, and specially to give him warning for the future. "Behold," says our Lord, "thou art made whole. Sin no more, lest a worse thing come unto thee."

In these words there is a clear recognition of the fact that the man's long infirmity was the result of his youthful sins. This, in one sense, is true of all sickness and suffering; they result from the violation of the laws of our physical being, and he who sins against these laws sins against God their author, and violation of law always exposes to punishment. How frequently do we see in daily life this truth sadly worked out in the lives of the sick and the suffering! How much force of meaning is thus given to that expression of the law of the perpetuating of evil, "Thou makest me to possess the iniquities of my youth" (Job xiii. 26), and that other declaration of Job, "His bones are full of the sin of his youth" (xx. 11)! For medical men will tell us with one voice that the larger part of the maladies of the human family are the results of youthful excesses and indiscretions, the open or secret violations of the laws by which God had hedged in and protected our health and happiness, but which passion, self-indulgence, waywardness, had caused us to break through, reaping at the time, perhaps, no immediate evil from our transgressions, but yet certainly laying up in store future evils that would surely vindicate the broken law.

This truth has forced itself even upon heathen minds. Cicero, in his "De Senectute," not only tells us that the loss of strength is more frequently the fault of youth than of old age, but he adds that a youth of sensuality and intemperance transmits to old age a worn-out, used-up body.

The author of Lacon (Colton), when he says that "the excesses of youth are bills drawn by Time, payable thirty years after date, with interest," only paraphrases the terse Latin proverb that we pay when old, for our sins when young.

Even when a man repents of his sins and becomes a new creature in Christ Jesus, breaking off from all former indulgences, he does not thereby secure immunity from the operation of this law; for while the religion of Jesus Christ saves the soul, it does not repair the wastes and inroads upon the body which sin has already made. The vices which had undermined the constitution before he became a Christian still show the gaps and weakness of it, even after he becomes a child of God through faith in Christ Jesus.

These thoughts are borne out by that other declaration of God's word, "His own iniquities shall take the wicked himself, and he shall be holden with the cords of his sin." We suffer for our own misdoings even on earth. We braid together by the strands of our little and almost unnoticed youthful sins, the cords which bind us so tightly about with pain and discomfort and remorse in middle life or old age. It is retributive justice finding us out on earth, and by its chastenings warning us to immediate repentance, to flee from the deeper and more enduring wrath that will, if unrepenting, overtake us in the world to come.

And then again these words of Jesus, "Sin no more, lest a worse thing come unto thee," imply that to sin afresh, after receiving signal mercies, is but to incur more grievous judgment. Surely it was a bad thing that thirty and eight years of this cripple's life had been made full of pain and misery, and had been rendered utterly useless by reason of his early sins; but bad as was that almost life-long suffering, wretched and degraded as he had become through helplessness and poverty, there was a "worse thing" yet in reserve if he again went back to his sins, "like a sow that was washed to her wallowing in the mire." For in sinning afresh, after receiving great blessing, the man commits a twofold wrong: he ignores the blessings received from their divine Author, and in spite of warnings, breaks away into new transgressions. Hence the moral force which he must necessarily put forth to do these things, in spite of blessings, in spite of warnings, in spite of the lashings of conscience, gives to him such an impetus, such a momentum, as it were, that he is carried beyond all his former bounds of guilt, and finds himself in new fields of sin, and under a deeper spell of evil. This truth our Lord illustrated with startling force, and in a manner which should awaken most serious consideration, when he speaks of the cast out devil returning again to the house whence he was ejected. "When he cometh back," saith our Lord, "he findeth it empty—swept and garnished; then goeth he and taketh to himself seven other spirits worse than the first, and they enter in and dwell there, and the last state of that man is worse than the first." We cannot too often call to mind these truths. Let us never forget that much—yea, probably (could we see the subtle connection), all—of our pains and sicknesses are directly or indirectly the result of our sins or the sins of our parents. "However unwilling we may be to receive this, bringing, as it does, God so near, and making retribution so real and so prompt a thing, yet it is true notwithstanding. As some eagle pierced with a shaft feathered from its own wing, so many a sufferer even in this present time sees and is compelled to acknowledge that his own sin fledged the arrow which has pierced him and brought him down." History, sacred and profane, abounds with illustrative instances of this truth, and each one can perhaps find still further confirmation in the experiences of his own life.

As soon as the man ascertained the name of his benefactor, he "departed and told the Jews that it was Jesus who had made him whole." Not as a heartless wretch wishing to betray, but as a grateful man anxious to make known the name and fame of Him who had done so great things unto him. The effect of this communication so stirred up this priestly party that they manifested at once a hatred which eagerly sought to catch him and slay him "because he had done these things on the Sabbath day."

According to the Levitical law (Ex. xxxi. 14, Num. xv. 35), the penalty of breaking the Sabbath was death by stoning. They regarded Jesus as having broken the Sabbath, and hence "they sought to slay him." But the violator of the Mosaic law could only be stoned to death judicially—*i. e.*, after a fair trial—and the witnesses of his guilt were to be the first to cast the death-dealing stones. But the power of life and death had been taken away from the Jews by their Roman masters, and as the rulers confessed to Pilate, "It is not lawful for us to put any one to death." What these enraged "Jews" wanted was, to wreak their vengeance on Jesus, whose words, whose works, whose life, was a daily reproach to them, a constant galling of their pride, their presumption, their pretended piety; and unable to brook his reproaches or to turn away the people from following him, they determined, if possible, by any means to get rid of him.

There could be no peace to the scribes and the Pharisees while he was alive. His very presence revealed all their darkness and iniquity, just as the presence of light makes visible all the foul and noisome things upon which it shines. Their rage had been excited against him from the time he made a scourge of small cords and cleansed the temple by driving out of it the sheep and oxen and the money-changers, and denouncing them as having made his "Father's house a den of thieves." From that hour their rancor knew no bounds. They hunted diligently for evidence to convict him of some great crime. They cared not what it was if it would only secure his destruction. Hence they sent Herodians "to entangle him in his talk" that they might accuse him to Herod of political crime; and hence by artful ways they sought to bring him into conflict with the great Sanhedrim that that powerful body might secure from Pilate his longed-for death. This was the spirit which now possessed these "Jews," and under the influence of which they sought to slay Him whose daily life and teaching were so obnoxious to them.

Jesus flinches not at their presence. He boldly confronts them and meets their objections by an argument of the most dignified and profound character.

This vindication of himself is found in John v. 17-47. Whether spoken on the Sabbath day in the temple, or afterward when arraigned perhaps before the lesser Sanhedrim on the judicial charge of breaking the Sabbath, we cannot tell. Whenever or wherever uttered, it is one of Christ's most sublime discourses, and constitutes a thorough defence of himself, first against the charge of Sabbath-breaking and secondly against the subsequent charge growing out of Jesus' refutation of the first—viz., blasphemy, "making himself equal with God."

As to the first charge, of breaking the Sabbath, God the Father, who ordained the Sabbath to commemorate his resting on the seventh day, not from fatigue, but from active creative effort, "worketh hitherto" in the upholding and conserving and governing the world which he made in six days, and thus ceaselessly doing good to all his creatures, and "I," his Son in all the divine fullness which that relation implies, "work"—work as he works in doing good, not in servile work for selfish ends, but in Godlike works for holy ends; not as a breaker of the law of the Sabbath, as if it required complete passiveness and abstinence from good deeds even, but as a true keeper of the law in the spirit of Him who gave the law—a spirit of ceaseless benevolence and love flowing out in active blessings, not for six days and then ceasing, but on the seventh day as well as on the sixth, because the work done was as holy as the day, and as the God who did it.

This line of defence, placing himself as "equal with God" in the right and purpose to work as the Father worked, so far from being accepted by these Judaists, was made the ground of the second charge against him of blasphemy, as thus "making himself equal with God." This second charge Jesus quickly meets by asserting his equality with God in "work" (verses 17, 19, 20), in the power to raise the dead (v. 21), in the power to judge the world (v. 22), in the honor which it behoved men to bestow (v. 23), in the power to give eternal life (v. 26). This claim to divine Messiahship by doing all the works that their longed-for Messiah was to do, he confirms by the specific testimony of John the Baptist (v. 32-35), the testimony of Moses (v. 45-47), the testimony of all the scriptures (v. 39), the testimony of his own miraculous works (v. 36-38), and in the witness of God the Father (v. 37).

To this triumphant and unanswerable vindication of himself, the Jews—the spiritual rulers of the people—could give no reply. John the Baptist, to whom they had appealed, was against them. Moses, in whom they trusted, was against them. The Scriptures, in which they sought eternal life, were against them. God, whom they claimed as their Father, was against them. Every ground of opposition to, and of condemnation of, Jesus was taken away by this discourse, and there remained only the deadly animosity of obdurate hearts and rebellious minds.

They who accused Jesus are now accused by him for their lack of the knowledge of the Scriptures, for their unwillingness to follow the lead of Moses, for their virtual rejection of the testimony of John the Baptist, and for their keeping away from Christ, the source of all spiritual life and light. They had arraigned him at their tribunal; he arraigns them at his. They had accused him of deeds worthy of temporal death;

he accuses them of deeds worthy of eternal death. There is something sublime in this attitude of Jesus in the presence of his accusers, quietly turning against them their own witnesses, convicting them of the very crimes which they charged against him, showing himself before them by many infallible proofs as their Messiah, claiming equality with God, and that "all men should honor him, even as they honor the Father." Had not Jesus been divine, this language would have been the most insufferable arrogance and blasphemy, but he was "God manifest in the flesh," and hence it is all true, and harmonizes with, and illustrates, both the human and the divine in the redeeming, the mediatorial and the judicial work of Christ.

SABBATH IN THE CORNFIELD.

CHAPTER VIII.

THE SABBATH IN THE CORN-FIELDS.

"At that time Jesus went on the Sabbath day through the corn; and his disciples were ahungered, and began to pluck the ears of corn, and to eat. But when the Pharisees saw it, they said unto him, Behold, thy disciples do that which is not lawful to do upon the Sabbath day. But he said unto them, Have ye not read what David did when he was ahungered, and they that were with him; how he entered into the house of God and did eat the shewbread, which was not lawful for him to eat, neither for them which were with him, but only for the priests? Or have ye not read in the law, how that on the Sabbath days the priests in the temple profane the Sabbath and are blameless? But I say unto you, That in this place is one greater than the temple. But if ye had known what this meaneth, I will have mercy, and not sacrifice, ye would not have condemned the guiltless. For the Son of man is Lord even of the Sabbath day. And when he was departed thence, he went into their Synagogue." MATT. xii. 1-9.

"For verily I say unto you, That whosoever shall say unto this mountain, Be thou removed, and be thou cast into the sea, and shall not doubt in his heart, but shall believe that those things which he saith shall come to pass, he shall have whatsoever he saith. Therefore I say unto you, What things soever ye desire, when ye pray, believe that ye receive them, and ye shall have them. And when ye stand praying, forgive, if ye have aught against any, that your Father also which is in heaven may forgive you your trespasses. But if ye do not forgive, neither will your Father which is in heaven forgive your trespasses. And they come again to Jerusalem; and as he was walking in the temple, there come to him the chief priests, and the scribes, and the elders, and say unto him, By what authority doest thou these things? and who gave thee this authority to do these things?" MARK xi. 23-28.

"And it came to pass on the second Sabbath after the first, that he went through the corn fields; and his disciples plucked the ears of corn and did eat, rubbing them in their hands. And certain of the Pharisees said unto them, Why do ye that which is not lawful to do on the Sabbath days? And Jesus answering them said, Have ye not read so much as this, what David did, when himself was ahungered, and they which were with him; how he went into the house of God, and did take and eat the shewbread, and gave also to them that were with him, which it is not lawful to eat but for the priests alone? And he said unto them, That the Son of man is Lord also of the Sabbath." LUKE vi. 1–5.

HE period referred to by the opening sentence of St. Matthew, "At that time," was when, after calling and commissioning his twelve disciples as recorded in the tenth chapter, Jesus "departed thence to teach and to preach in their cities"—*i. e.*, it was during one of his missionary circuits among the towns on the western shore of the Sea of Galilee.

St. Luke marks it as "the second Sabbath after the first," being a "great Sabbath," as it was the first Sabbath "of a year that stood second in a sabbatical cycle." On this Sabbath day, as Jesus and his disciples passed through the corn-fields (not what we in America term such, filled with maize or Indian corn, but fields of wheat and barley, which in that country at that time, being in all probability about the first of April, were then just ripening into harvest), his disciples, being hungry, "began to pluck the ears of corn and did eat, rubbing them in their hands" to remove the husk. This it was lawful for them to do, for the direction in Deut. xxiii. 25 reads, "When thou comest into the standing corn of thy neighbor, then thou mayest pluck the ears with thy hand; but thou shalt not move a sickle unto thy neighbor's standing corn." In that country, it must be remembered, the fields are not enclosed with fences, as with us, but are separated one from the other by certain stones, stakes, ridges or ditches which constitute the "land-marks" of the several owners. The effect of this is, to make a whole plain or valley, preceding harvest-time, appear as one vast unenclosed field, and never did that verse of David's in which he says, in order to indicate fertility and luxuriance, "The valleys also stand so thick with corn that they shall laugh and sing" (lxv. 13, Pr. Bk. vers.), come out to our mind with such pastoral beauty as when, looking down over the large corn-fields just waiting for the sickle, we saw them rolling to and fro in the wind with that billowy motion which, like a gleeful smile, dimpled and rippled over the waving grain, while the rustling of the stalks and leaves swaying in the breeze rose up like the voice of singing. To this harmless act of our Lord's disciples, and done for the purpose of satisfying their hunger, the Pharisees objected because done on the Sabbath day.

One of the laws of the Pharisees, as subsequently embodied in the Talmud, was, "He that reapeth corn on the Sabbath to the quantity of a fig is guilty; and plucking corn is as reaping, and whosoever plucketh up anything growing is guilty under the notion of reaping."

In reply to this pharisaical objection, our Lord justifies the act of his disciples in what they did by citing cases and principles which entirely set aside their rigorous literalism, and placed the day and its observance on their true basis. "Have ye not read," he asks, "what David did when he had need and was anhungered, and they that were with him, how he went into the house of God in the days of Abiathar the high priest, and did take and eat the shewbread which is not lawful to eat but for the priests, and gave also to them that were with him?" The reference here is to the transaction recorded in 1 Samuel xxi. 1, et seq., when David, fleeing from the persecution of Saul, went to the sacerdotal city of Nob, situated in the tribe of Benjamin, and there begged of the high priest the shewbread (the "bread of faces" as it was called) for himself and hungry companions.

The shewbread consisted of twelve cakes or loaves made of fine flour and set "in two rows, six on a row, upon the pure table before the Lord, and thou shalt put pure frankincense upon each row that it may be on the bread for a memorial, even an offering made by fire unto the Lord. Every Sabbath he shall set it in order before the Lord continually. And it shall be Aaron's and his sons', and they shall eat it in the holy place, for it is most holy unto him of the offerings of the Lord made by fire." Lev. xxiv. 5–9. At the time of the weekly renewal of the shewbread the incense upon each row was burned before the Lord, and the loaves were eaten by the priests in the temple.

It was this shewbread, just removed from the table to give place to the fresh and hot, which, in his extreme necessity, David asked for and received, and of which he and his hungry men partook. Though ordinarily unlawful for him to eat it, as he was not of the Levitical priesthood, yet his pressing need made it right both for the priest to give and for him to take the hallowed loaves, because it was better to prolong life and meet the imperious demands of hunger at the expense of a ceremonial law, than by keeping the law of sacrifice subject man to suffering, and thus break the higher law of mercy.

From the narrative in Samuel we may rightly infer that it was on the Sabbath that David and his men went into the sanctuary and ate this bread, thus intensifying the crime, if crime it was; but our Lord showed conclusively, by citing this case with approval, that neither David nor the priest had violated the spirit of the ceremonial law in the transaction, and that there were human necessities which rightfully set aside all Levitical regulations.

Rising from a personal and exceptional act, our Lord cites another case of a general character, where the apparent violation of the sabbatic law is done, not by a few lay people, but by all the priests; not in Nob alone, but in Jerusalem the holy city; not in a humble Synagogue, but in the Temple itself, and that, too, in the very act by which they profess to worship Jehovah.

"Or have ye not read in the law how that on

THE TRANSFIGURATION.

the Sabbath days the priests in the temple profane the Sabbath and are blameless? But I say unto you, That in this place is one greater than the temple. But if ye had known what this meaneth, I will have mercy and not sacrifice, ye would not have condemned the guiltless."

St. Matthew only records these words of our Lord, yet they are most significant and pungent in their bearing on the question before him. As if he had said, You say no burdens shall be borne, no fire kindled, no utensil handled, no manual labor performed, yet the priests in the discharge of their duties in the temple carry in wood, lay it on the altar, slay the victims, kindle fires, handle the sacrificial knives, carve up the offered lambs and goats, and therefore, according to your views, profane or secularize and make unholy the Sabbath; yet you say that they are blameless, for the maxim of the Jews in reference to this very temple-work was, that there is no Sabbath in the temple, and that the temple sanctified the work. Indeed, so far from remitting labor on this day because it was the Sabbath, the labor was doubled by reason of the double sacrifices which were required by the Levitical law (Num. xxviii. 9, 10). Yet they "are blameless," yourselves being judges, for you never thought of arraigning a priest as a Sabbath-breaker because he killed and flayed and quartered a burnt-offering, and you never thought of interdicting the temple-worship because it required double toil and service of its ministers on the seventh day. Now, then, if the fact that these works are blameless because they were done in and for the temple, the temple thus giving sanctity to the act, so I, who am here with you "in this place," am "greater than the temple," and can give to works done by me, or with my permission, that sanctity, that they shall not profane, but hallow, the Sabbath, for being done by or for me, they are lifted out of the level of secular things and partake of the holiness of the person they are designed to serve. If the temple, therefore, makes the priests blameless, I, who am "greater than the temple," hold my disciples blameless; for not only have they done no more than David did, satisfying hunger by doing what was technically and traditionally unlawful, but they have done their works as the priests did their service, for the Lord of the temple himself, now standing before you.

To understand in what respect Jesus was "greater than the temple," we must consider a moment what the temple was in his eye. Without going into the structure of the tabernacle in the wilderness, or the temple which succeeded it, and which loomed up like a cloud of glory on Mt. Moriah, or marking their numerous typical relations to, and prefigurings of, Christ, it will suffice to say, as St. Paul does in the Epistle to the Hebrews (ix. 9–12), that it "was a figure for the time then present, in which were offered both gifts and sacrifices, that could not make him that did the service perfect as pertaining to the conscience; which stood only in meats and drinks, and divers washings, and carnal ordinances, imposed on them until the time of reformation. But Christ being come an high priest of good things to come, by a greater and more perfect tabernacle, not made with hands, that is to say, not of this building, neither by the blood of goats and calves, but by his own blood he entered in once into the holy place, having obtained eternal redemption for us." The temple, then, in its structure, its ritual, its sacrifices, its priests, was designed to present to the eye and mind of the Jew the one great doctrine of the atonement of sin through vicarious blood—viz., the unforfeited life or blood of the guiltless and the innocent, shed for the forfeited life or blood of the guilty and the sinning. The temple was the embodiment of this atoning idea. It was God's thought of mercy to man, put into shape and made visible before the nation for hundreds of years by means of priest and sacrifice and incense and holy and most holy place, and all the rites, personalities and buildings which made up what we express by one word, "the temple." In this aspect the things of the temple were, as the Epistle to the Hebrews states, "patterns of things in the heavens," "figures of the true," "a shadow of good things to come, and not the very image of the things." But Christ was the substance which forecast this shadow. He was the antitype of which these earthly structures and emblems were "the figures." He was the original of that of which the temple was but an imperfect "pattern." Christ, in his person and his work, was not only all that the temple adumbrated, but infinitely more. Hence he speaks of himself as a "temple" in that passage which so puzzled the Jews, "Destroy this temple, and in three days will I raise it again," but "he spake of the temple of his body." If the temple, then, was but a shadowing forth of what the Messiah should be and do, the Messiah who was thus prefigured, or who thus cast this shadow, must be greater than the temple, so that Jesus, knowing that he was the Messiah and having declared it openly in his conversation with the woman of Samaria at Jacob's well, could truly say, as he stood before his carping enemies, "In this place is one greater than the temple."

If those who served on the Sabbath about the earthly, the material temple, did so and were blameless, those, therefore, who ministered to and about him the living Temple, "greater than the temple" which sanctifies priestly service, can supply their necessities, and make themselves more ready to discharge their duties, and also be blameless.

Jesus then tells them, "If ye had known what this meaneth, I will have mercy and not sacrifice, ye would not have condemned the guiltless." This is a quotation from the prophet Hosea (vi. 6): "For I desired mercy and not sacrifice," placing the higher value on the inward affection of the heart and not on the outward and visible act. It is couched in one of those forms of Hebrew negation where the use of the negative (not) is not designed to express that the "sacrifice" is unnecessary or improper, but to intensify that with which sacrifice is contrasted, "mercy," and to show that in the comparison of the two "mercy" will take the supremacy. Thus "sacrifice," good in itself, ordained by God, held a lower place in God's view than "mercy," that emotion of a tender, loving, considerate soul.

The "mercy" which the Pharisees showed was limited to external acts—feeding the hungry, blowing a trumpet before them when they gave alms, and such-like. There was in their doing these outward and visible things no mercy, for all their acts were done "to be seen of men;" the true spirit of kindness and charity was absent. So our Lord says to these Jews, If you had only known this truth (brought out so clearly by Hosea and Micah, vi. 6, 8), you would have put a kindly interpretation on this act of my disciples, and not treated as guilty those whom I pronounce guiltless. It is the absence of this spirit among Christians now, which is productive of so much evil and faultfinding and dissensions. It is this spirit of legalism ever striving against the spirit of a merciful liberalism which is doing so much to check the growth of the Church and bind upon the conscience "burdens grievous to be borne," which tithes anise and mint and cummin and neglects the weightier matters of the law, judgment, mercy and truth. It is a harsh, technical, faultfinding spirit. It looks solely to "the letter of the law" and the outside of the ceremonial. But the law of mercy looks at the state of the heart, and busies itself more about the aspect of the soul toward God than about its appearance toward men. Micah brings out this truth with great force when he asks, "Wherewith shall I come before the Lord and bow myself before the high God? Shall I come before him with burnt-offerings, with calves of a year old? Will the Lord be pleased with thousands of rams or with ten thousands of rivers of oil? Shall I give my first-born for my transgression, the fruit of my body for the sin of my soul? He hath showed thee, O man! what is good; and what doth the Lord require of thee but to do justly and to love mercy and to walk humbly with thy God?"

These grand utterances of the old prophet,

seven hundred years before Christ, find their full echo and response in the equally strong declaration of St. Paul: "Though I speak with the tongues of men and of angels, and have not charity (that inner love of the soul out of which mercy grows), I am become as sounding brass or a tinkling cymbal; and though I have the gift of prophecy and understand all mysteries and all knowledge, and though I have all faith, so that I could remove mountains, and have not charity, I am nothing. And though I give all my goods to feed the poor, and though I give my body to be burned, and have not charity, I am nothing." What strides onward the Church would make if ministers and people would only cultivate more of this "mercy" which "rejoiceth against judgment," and would put on this charity which the apostle tells us "is the very bond of perfectness"! for mercy would assimilate our character to that of God, and charity (love) is "the fulfilling of the law."

After speaking this deserved rebuke to these unmerciful Pharisees, our Lord enunciates the truth, "The Son of man is Lord even of the Sabbath day." This assertion is recorded by the three writers, Matthew, Mark and Luke, and nearly in the same words. In making this assertion he wanted his hearers to know that he regarded himself as "the Lord of the Sabbath," and could, out of himself, give the laws which should regulate its observance, and therefore that nothing that he did could break an institution of which he was Lord or Ruler.

St. Mark prefixes this declaration with another—viz., "The Sabbath was made for man, not man for the Sabbath." Judging from the pre-eminence given by the scribes and Pharisees to the fourth commandment, and the excessive care shown in fencing it around with all kinds of restrictions, so that the memory could neither retain them nor the people fully observe them, it was needful that our Lord should take just such a common-sense view of the Sabbath as he does take in these words. So unjustly had they magnified this law, not only out of proportion to the others, but in contravention of the others, that they declared, "He who shall duly observe all the rites and customs of the Sabbath shall obtain the pardon of all his sins, even though he hath been guilty of idolatry." The Sabbath was thus bound hand and foot in the grave-clothes of stringent traditions. Its original and benignant purpose had been overlooked in their rabbinical glosses, and it was time that the order should go forth from the Lord of the Sabbath, "Loose it and let it go," that it might stand forth untrammeled by the swathings and bandages of those scribes who had on this, as on many other subjects, taught for doctrines the commandments of men, and thus "made the word of God of none effect through their traditions." The Sabbath, or a rest one day in seven, was made and ordained by God for man's physical, mental and moral good. It was to give him rest from earthly toils and cares, and time for heavenly thoughts and acts. It was to be, not a burden, but a comfort. It was to be a means to an end; that end man's highest earthly and eternal good. "Wherever, therefore, the keeping of the Sabbath in the way prescribed, instead of promoting would frustrate that end, it was more honored in the breach than in the observance. It was never to be regarded as itself an end. Apart from the physical, social, moral and religious benefits to be thereby realized, there was no merit in painfully doing this one thing, or rigorously abstaining from that other. The Sabbath was made to serve man, but not man to serve, or be a slave to, the Sabbath. And just because it is an institution which, when rightly used, is so eminently fitted to minister to man's present and eternal good, the Son of man, who came not to be ministered unto, but to minister as the Head of our humanity, to render to it the greatest of all services and to take all other servants of it under his care and keeping, would show himself to be "Lord also of the Sabbath."

It is worthy of note here, in passing, that with one exception (Acts vii. 56), our Lord only speaks of himself as the "Son of man." It is a term used by none of the apostles, but fifty different times by Jesus himself, as if it was the favorite title by which he would designate himself. It is a name which the prophet Daniel (vii. 13) gives to the Messiah, and hence was a name recognized by the Jews as a designation of the Messiah. As the phrase, "Son of God," when applied to Jesus, meant the full and perfect communication to him of the divine nature, with all its attributes and functions, so that we could truly say as St. Paul does, "In him dwelleth all the fullness of the Godhead bodily," so the phrase, "Son of man," when used by him, indicated the full and perfect communication to him of the human nature, with all its attributes and functions, sin only excepted, so that he is indeed "the second Adam, the Lord from heaven." In his human nature he "was made of a woman—made under the law," "for verily he took not on him the nature of angels, but he took on him the seed of Abraham, wherefore in all things it behoved him to be made like unto his brethren," and he was therefore made in the likeness of men. It is a term that thus identifies Christ with the men whom he came to save. He has taken to himself our humanity. He has exalted and glorified it, and lifted it up out of the depths into which sin had degraded it, and brought us into the light and liberty of the children of God;—while it also shows, that as the Son of man he was the highest and fullest embodiment of humanity—man without sin, man perfectly holy, man with no physical defect, no mental idiosyncrasies, no class, national or religious prejudices; man in the full, rounded and complete development of all his mental and moral faculties, incorporating in himself all the glories and perfections of a sinless and unfallen manhood; the ideal of what man would have been had he not sinned; the pattern of what man ought to be on earth;—the type of what man will be in the heavenly regeneration.

As "the Son of man" gathering up into himself all the interests of our common humanity and ruling over everything that bore upon its welfare here, and destiny hereafter, he had the right of Lordship and sovereignty over an institution "made for man"—the Sabbath—and hence could do with it whatever his holy will pleased without breaking its sanctity or enfeebling its power. He is the Arbiter of his own ordinance, the interpreter of his own law, and he therefore, by the bold declaration that "the Sabbath was made for man," reinstates it in its primitive design, and re-enforces its claims by his own authority and example. It becomes no longer, under this interpretation of Jesus, a day of burdensome exactions and tedious ceremonies, hampering the free spirit and fettering every natural emotion by traditional restrictions or the tightened ligatures of pharisaic formalism; but it is made a day of joy, of freedom from servile work, of social and domestic happiness, of personal and private communion with God, of public worship with the assemblies of

God's people, of doing works of mercy and charity, of reading and meditating on God's word and works. There is nothing rigid or straitlaced about it. It is enfranchised from all Jewish glosses, and man is called upon to use and enjoy this Sabbath in a manner that shall at once glorify and honor the Lord of the Sabbath, and secure the highest welfare of man for whom this Sabbath was made.

In reference to what is called the Sabbath question, we should ever keep these two cardinal facts before us, that Jesus is the Lord of the Sabbath, and that the Sabbath was made for man.

The first fact being true, it follows that we must use the Sabbath for the service and glory of him who is its Lord; otherwise we fail to recognize his Lordship over it, and set at naught his divine authority.

It follows further that the hours of the Sabbath are Jesus' special gift, and we must do nothing in its hours that will contravene its sacredness, such as appropriating them to mere secular purposes or the advancement of secular ends.

It follows still further that the example of

Christ, in so far as it is applicable to us, must be our pattern. He employed its hours in being in the places of worship, whether Synagogue or Temple, where he happened to be in ministering to the sick and suffering; in preaching and teaching the gospel of the kingdom; in consoling the afflicted, and in partaking of the social hospitality offered to him. He swept away with one wave of his hand the cumbrous traditions which had encrusted themselves about this fourth commandment, and because he did so he involved himself in frequent conflicts with the scribes and Pharisees, who judged his actions according to the letter of their traditions, rather than by the spirit of the law itself.

The second fact being true, that "the Sabbath was made for man," it follows that man ought to regard it as a divinely ordained institution for his special enjoyment and blessing. It is an ordinance indissolubly bound up with man's best and highest interests. It was made to give him what, but for this day of rest, he would not have—a periodical remission of work, a periodical season of worship. It is a day for him to put the world aside and bring heaven into view; to let the body rest, that the soul may wing its way upward before the throne; that soiled and begrimed, as it were, by his six days' work, he might wash off the earthiness from his spirit and bring his heart into the house of God, to hear the word of God, to engage in the worship of God and to listen to the preaching of the ambassador of God.

It would be impossible to tell a tithe of the blessings which result to man from a right enjoyment of this Lord's day. Are we slaves to business all the week? This rest-day enables us to stand up the Lord's freemen. Is our mind all the week immersed in worldly cares and studies? On this rest-day we fling open the window of the soul and let the light of the celestial city stream in upon it. It is a day which comes to us laden with blessings. It brings in its hands all good things and all lovable things and all holy things for our souls and for our bodies. It offers us rest, retirement, spiritual refreshment, a feast of fat things in God's earthly house. It invites us to holy domestic and social gatherings where all the finer and nobler feelings of our nature can have free exercise. It shuts the gate upon the world, and swings open for a time the gate of pearl that we may look in upon the glories of the New Jerusalem. He who spends the Lord's day in a manner that will honor the Lord of the Sabbath stands, as it were, in the antechamber of heaven, and is thereby becoming more and more meet for the inheritance of the saints in light and for "the rest that remaineth for the people of God."

CHAPTER IX.

CHRIST HEALING THE WITHERED HAND IN THE SYNAGOGUE ON THE SABBATH.

"And when he was departed thence, he went into their Synagogue; and, behold, there was a man which had his hand withered. And they asked him, saying, Is it lawful to heal on the Sabbath days? that they might accuse him. And he said unto them, What man shall there be among you that shall have one sheep, and if it fall into a pit on the Sabbath day, will he not lay hold on it and lift it out? How much then is a man better than a sheep? Wherefore it is lawful to do well on the Sabbath days. Then saith he to the man, Stretch forth thine hand. And he stretched it forth, and it was restored whole, like as the other. Then the Pharisees went out, and held a council against him, how they might destroy him." MATT. xii. 9-14.

"And he entered again into the Synagogue; and there was a man there which had a withered hand. And they watched him, whether he would heal him on the Sabbath day, that they might accuse him. And he saith unto the man which had the withered hand, Stand forth. And he saith unto them, Is it lawful to do good on the Sabbath days, or to do evil? to save life, or to kill? But they held their peace. And when he had looked round about on them with anger, being grieved for the hardness of their hearts, he saith unto the man, Stretch forth thine hand. And he stretched it out; and his hand was restored whole as the other. And the Pharisees went forth, and straightway took counsel with the Herodians against him, how they might destroy him." MARK iii. 1-6.

"And it came to pass also on another Sabbath that he entered into the Synagogue and taught; and there was a man whose right hand was withered. And the scribes and Pharisees watched him, whether he would heal on the Sabbath day, that they might find an accusation against him. But he knew their thoughts, and said to the man which had the withered hand, Rise up, and stand forth in the midst. And he arose and stood forth. Then said Jesus unto them, I will ask you one thing: Is it lawful on the Sabbath days to do good, or to do evil? to save life, or to destroy it? And looking round about upon them all, he said unto the man, Stretch forth thy hand. And he did so, and his hand was restored whole as the other. And they were filled with madness, and communed one with another what they might do to Jesus." LUKE vi. 6–11.

HE narrative of this Sabbath is placed by the three Evangelists in close connection with the Sabbath which we have just considered. Still, it is entirely distinct, as St. Luke tells us that it was upon "another Sabbath."

Where the Synagogue was is not stated, though it was doubtless in or near Capernaum. From the tenor of the language used we can infer that, knowing our Lord would visit this Synagogue on this day, the scribes and Pharisees had brought there a man whose right hand was withered, as a bait to catch him in some work of healing, for it is stated that "they watched him whether he would heal on the Sabbath day," not that they might applaud him for his work of mercy, but "that they might find an accusation against him." The man with the withered right hand was evidently a prominent object, and they inferred from our Lord's ready exercise of mercy that he would most likely display it on his behalf. Jesus knew their evil thoughts, the aim and purpose of their plans, and as if to anticipate any movement on their part, and to make the transaction the more conspicuous, he said to the man, "Rise up and stand forth in the midst, and he arose and stood forth."

All was now excitement and expectation. The looks of the audience were passing rapidly from Jesus to the man, and from the man to the rulers of the Synagogue, in the consciousness that a great event was at hand.

Knowing, doubtless, our Lord's purpose in telling the man to "rise up and stand forth," they put to him the question, "Is it lawful to heal on the Sabbath day?" with the design of entrapping him into an answer which would furnish the ground of accusation against him as a breaker of the law of Moses. He, however, as St. Luke tells us, "knew their thoughts;" their wicked hearts and perverted minds lay bare and open before his piercing eyes, so that neither their feigned courtesy nor their hypocritical righteousness deceived him. And so, after the man had at Christ's command risen from his place and gone into the open space in the Synagogue where all could see his withered and useless arm, he replied to the question by saying, "I will also ask you one thing: is it lawful on the Sabbath days to do good or to do evil, to save life or to destroy it?" The question itself carried its own answer, but without waiting for them to reply, he proceeds to illustrate his meaning by an appeal to their own experience in the common transactions of that sheep-raising country. "What man shall there be among you that shall have one sheep, and if it fall into a pit on the Sabbath day, will he not lay hold on it and lift it out? How much, then, is a man better than a sheep? Wherefore it is lawful to do well on the Sabbath days." What argument could be clearer, stronger, more convincing, than this? It was an appeal to their common-sense view of things, and to their pecuniary interests, which they could not gainsay, and so it is recorded of them that "they held their peace." They had nothing even plausible to object to such a putting of the truth, and so kept silence. But it was not the silence of assent, but the sullen silence of conscious defeat. They were baffled, but not convinced, and He who read their inmost thoughts knew the evil feelings that were roused within them by this thwarting of their well-laid plot, and hence he "turned and looked upon them with anger, being grieved for the hardness of their hearts."

This is the only place in which it is said that our Lord was angry. Yet, in saying that he "looked upon them with anger," we must not attach to it those ideas which we have of man's anger.

Anger which excites evil passions against the peace, the comfort, the life, of persons, which leads to words of wrath and deeds of violence, which stirs up enmity and revenge, which hurries one out of self-control into hasty and foolish actions, and which leaves its sad virulence behind,—such anger is sinful. But no such anger as this ever took possession of Jesus.

On the other hand, there is an anger which is just and sinless—an anger against sinful deeds, purposes, characters; an anger which is but righteous indignation against ungodly words and works, such as the apostle speaks of when he says, "Be ye angry and sin not." When St. Mark speaks of Jesus being angry, he means that his holy mind was deeply disturbed as he saw with his omniscient eye the evil thoughts and purposes of his enemies against himself, and therefore against man's Redeemer, and consequently against man's highest and eternal interests. It was at the sin which lay in the hearts of these men, and which broke out so fiercely in their words and acts, that he was angry—not at the poor sinners, but at that which made them such. "Indeed, with Him who was at once perfect love and perfect holiness, grief for the sinner must ever go hand in hand with anger against the sin; and this anger, which with us is in danger of becoming a turbid thing, of passing into anger against the man who is God's creature, instead of being anger against the sin which is the devil's corruption of God's creature, with him was perfectly pure, for it is not the agitation of the waters, but the sediment at the bottom, which troubles and defiles them, and where no sediment is, no impurity will follow on their agitation."

With this anger was mingled grief—"being grieved for the hardness of their hearts." Sinful anger never could mingle itself with holy grief, and this grief was holy because it was excited by seeing the hard, callous, impenetrable hearts of these men, who, while professing to keep the law in its letter, were breaking it constantly in spirit, who were mistaking shadows for the substance, and who were thus "blind leaders of the blind," remaining willfully blind when they might see, and refusing to come to the light "lest their deeds should be made manifest that they are out of God."

After surveying the audience with this all-comprehending look of blended anger and grief—a look which they all saw and felt—he said to the man, "Stretch forth thine hand." There was here no manipulating of the hand, no touch, no rubbings, no embrocations, but a simple direction to the man to do what, under other circumstances, it would have been impossible to do; and in doing as he was bid, in stretching it forth, it was restored whole as the other. The cure was instantaneous. So surprising an act of mercy, wrought so conspicuously in their midst, beyond all possible cavil as to its being effected by other agencies than by the word of Jesus, ought to have called out their admiration and praise. So far from it that St. Luke says that "they were filled with madness." The pent-up rage excited by his foiling all attempts to entangle him in his talk or works, and the conscious rebuke which they felt at his look and his words, and the fearlessness of Jesus which quailed not before their scrutiny, and stopped not in his works of mercy because they objected to his healing on the Sabbath, now burst forth with volcanic force. The words are emphatic, "filled with madness." Their hearts were overflowing with hate, rancor, disappointment, mortified pride, conscious guilt, so that they were beside themselves with rage. There was no room in their bosoms for a single feeling of kindness or mercy. In the great outburst of indignation all other emotions were absorbed, and to give efficacy to their rage and wreak their vengeance on their holy Victim was now the one aim and purpose of the maddened Pharisees.

To this end they "communed" first "one with another" as to what had best now be done, and then, calling together the Herodians, "took counsel against him how they might destroy him."

The Herodians were a body of men among the Jews who were the political partisans of Herod Antipas. This Herod, who married Herodias, his brother Philip's wife, beheaded John the Baptist; and to him Pilate sent our Lord on the day of his crucifixion. Aiming at higher power, he was banished to Lugdunum (Lyons), and died in exile about A. D. 40.

The Jews, as a people, chafed under the Roman yoke; and the Galileans particularly, a rough, easily excited and turbulent people, often rose up against the local Roman rulers, and were as often put down and reduced to still more galling bondage by the Roman soldiers. It was a stigma upon a Jew to point to him as a partisan of Herod, the tool of the Roman emperor. It was like deserting the standard of the lion of the tribe of Judah and ranging himself under the *labarum* of a heathen empire. It was a virtual confession of the failure of all Messianic prophecies and Messianic hopes, a sort of giving up in despair that, after all, the long-promised One, who was the hope of Israel, would not appear, and that it was best to accept the present order of things even though it placed a heathen governor over the royal generation of Jacob. The Herodians, as the upholders of heathen royalty in opposition to their old theocracy, and the supporters of a foreign prince

"Herod demands of the scribes where Christ should be born."

rather than a prince of the house of Judah, were shunned by the scribes and Pharisees, who decried them as infidels and profane, as willing for selfish and political ends to sacrifice all that was dear to the Jew, if the favor and protection of Rome might thereby be secured.

Notwithstanding this deep-rooted aversion of the rulers of the Jews to this political sect, we find now a ready coalescence with them on the part of the scribes and Pharisees in the common cause of destroying Jesus.

To get rid of Jesus they were willing for a time to sink all antipathies and opposition, and to use even the detested Herodians, if they might relieve themselves of the presence and teaching of the still more despised Nazarene. On a later occasion, toward the last days of our Lord's life, we find the Pharisees again making the same coalition, when "they sent out unto him their disciples with the Herodians" that "they might entangle him in his talk." Matt. xxii. 16.

How this shows the intensity of their opposition to our dear Lord! They were indeed "filled with madness." In seeking the aid of the Herodians they doubtless hoped to find something in the words or works of Jesus that might, by a forced interpretation, be made to show that he was disloyal to the powers that be—something that would bring him under the surveillance and condemnation of the Roman authorities. This is evident from the question which the Herodians put to him in their interview with him shortly before his death. With mock reverence and hypocritical words of courtesy they come to him, "saying, Master, we know that thou art true and teachest the way of God in truth, neither carest thou for any man, for thou regardest not the person of men. Tell us, therefore, what thinkest thou? Is it lawful to give tribute unto Cæsar or not?" Here was presented to him a dilemma on one or the other horn of which the Herodians felt sure that they would impale him; for if he answered, No, it is not lawful to give tribute to Cæsar, they could at once accuse him to the Romans as a seditionist and a refuser of tribute, which constituted a grave political crime punishable with death. If he said, Yes, it is lawful to give tribute, then they would accuse him of being a traitor to the Jewish theocracy, an enemy to Jewish independence and a supporter of Roman ascendency, which would destroy all his influence with the people. Our Lord "perceived their wickedness, and said, Why tempt ye me, hypocrites?" They could not so disguise their minds by honeyed words and flattering compliments as to hide from Him "who knew what was in man" the hypocrisy of these questions, and hence he reveals them to themselves as hypocrites, and makes them conscious of their duplicity before he answers their catching question. The manner of his reply is a marvel of wisdom. He calls for a piece of the "tribute money," not the Jewish shekel, but a Roman denarius or penny, the money in which the tax was paid and which had stamped on it Cæsar's image, and sometimes heathen emblems and superscriptions. Holding this before them, he simply asked, "Whose is this image and superscription?" They say unto him, "Cæsar's." Then saith he unto them, "Render unto Cæsar the things which are Cæsar's," as if he had said, The current coin of your country is Cæsar's, and its circulation, displacing as it did, for nearly all purposes except that of the temple-service, the Jewish coin, proves your subjection to Cæsar and his right to levy tribute. But if our Lord had stopped here, he would have at once been accused by the Pharisees of siding with the Herodians, and so been brought into disgrace with all pious Jews. He does not, however, stop, but adds the markedly significant words, "and unto God the things that are God's." As made in the image of God and bearing, as it were, his superscription, "Holy to the Lord," give yourselves to him as the tribute due to your divine Creator and King.

These two instances in which the proud Pharisees made common cause with the hated Herodians for the purpose of destroying Jesus evince the animosity of both parties, and their readiness to forget lifelong hatreds if they may but slay their common enemy.

Such is always the attitude which sin takes toward holiness. The presence of holiness invariably draws out the opposition of sin. Sin hates light, "neither cometh to the light lest its deeds should be made manifest that they are not of God." Holiness is spiritual light. It is a revealing power, making known on the one hand the beauty and excellency of God, and on the other the heinousness of sin as "that abominable thing which God hateth." They ever have been, and must necessarily ever continue to be, antagonistic. In the case before us Jesus had done nothing which was wrong. He had, indeed, gone contrary to the traditions of their elders, but his vindication of himself had completely silenced their lips. He had done no works but those of mercy. He had spoken no words but those of purity and compassion. He had allied himself to no sect, political or theocratic. Why then this enmity, this continual plotting against his life, as if he were a robber or a murderer? It was because of the hardness of their hearts and the blindness of their eyes, which refused to recognize his Messianic claims, though fortified by such a holy life, such godly wisdom and such supernatural works.

The same effect, though not manifesting itself in the same way, is seen now, as it was then. The holding up of Jesus, and the truth as it is in Jesus; the declaring that unless men believe in him they will be damned; that "he that hath the Son hath life, and he that hath not the Son hath not life, but the wrath of God abideth on him;"—these truths, when read in the Bible or proclaimed from the pulpit or uttered in private, will always arouse the hatred of the unrenewed heart and provoke deadly opposition to the Lord Jesus. The spirit that now ruleth in the hearts of the children of disobedience is not going to yield its claims, or its domicil, without stout opposition. Hence, any attack upon the heart under the influence of sin by truth, wakes up the enmity of that heart to God, and manifests its deeply-seated guilt.

What a comment is this on sin! It hates God, the great and glorious Being who is the author of every good and perfect gift. It hates Jesus, the holy One of God—holy, harmless, undefiled—who, when on earth, went about doing good and gave his life a ransom for many. It hates the Holy Ghost, the Lord and giver of life, the spirit of truth and holiness, the renewer and sanctifier of the heart. It hates God's word, which reveals his nature, man's sin and the world's Saviour. It hates God's Church, the blessed company of all faithful people, with its divine ordinances of grace. It hates God's ministers, the heralds commissioned by him to preach, saying, "Repent, for the kingdom of heaven is at hand." It hates all good men whose daily lives bud and blossom with grace and bring forth the fruit of the Spirit. There is nothing good and holy and divine which sin does not hate, and would not, if it could, destroy. What it cannot destroy it will seek to defile; what it cannot defile it will vilify; what it cannot vilify it will mock or counterfeit. It is an ever-active hatred, and in the individual man begins with the first dawnings of spiritual life, and follows the soul through all its pilgrimage days until death ends the conflict. Yet all who are out of Christ, who have not a lively faith in him, and whose life is not answerable to this faith, are servants of sin, slaves of the prince of the power of the air, "the spirit that now ruleth in the hearts of the children of disobedience." What a master to serve! a fallen angel cast down from heaven. What a service to engage in! a daily slavery in working against everything good and holy. What wages to receive at the end of this servile toil! death! "The wages of sin is death."

So soon as our Lord perceived the spirit of these Pharisees, and that they had taken counsel with the Herodians against him, "he withdrew himself with his disciples." His time was not yet come. He would not, by remaining and contending with these adversaries, precipitate events, and hence went down to the seaside and thus thwarted their murderous plans.

This narrative teaches us the blinding nature of sin. It causes the eye of the mind to look at the highest moral beauties and see no beauty in them; to behold the most holy characters and mark no excellences therein; and attributes to mean and unworthy motives the most exemplary and charitable acts. Grace long resisted is sure to beget judicial blindness, for God's Spirit will not always strive with man.

This narrative also teaches us that the heart of Jesus is grieved by the perversity of men. When Christ exhibits himself to men in his word, his Church, his sacraments, his Spirit, and they reject him and seek only how to rid themselves of him, then is the holy heart of the Saviour grieved at the hardness and impenitency of those whom he came to save, but who say, "Away with him." "We will not have this man to reign over us." May God save us from the doom of rejecting an offered, loving, bleeding, divine Saviour!

CHAPTER X.

THE SECOND SABBATH IN NAZARETH.

"And when he was come into his own country, he taught them in their Synagogue, insomuch that they were astonished and said, Whence hath this man this wisdom, and these mighty works? Is not this the carpenter's son? is not his mother called Mary? and his brethren, James, and Joses, and Simon, and Judas? And his sisters, are they not all with us? Whence then hath this man all these things? And they were offended in him But Jesus said unto them, A prophet is not without honor save in his own country, and in his own house. And he did not many mighty works there because of their unbelief.". MATT. xiii. 54–58.

• "And he went out from thence and came into his own country, and his disciples follow him. And when the Sabbath day was come, he began to teach in the Synagogue; and many hearing him were astonished, saying, From whence hath this man these things? and what wisdom is this which is given unto him, that even such mighty works are wrought by his hands? Is not this the carpenter, the son of Mary, the brother of James and Joses, and of Juda and Simon? and are not his sisters here with us? And they were offended at him. But Jesus said unto them, A prophet is not without honor, but in his own country, and among his own kin, and in his own house. And he could there do no mighty work, save that he laid his hands upon a few sick folk and healed them. And he marveled because of their unbelief. And he went round about the villages, teaching." MARK vi. 1–6.

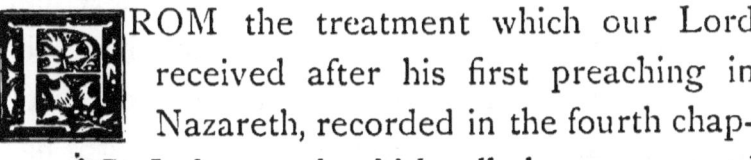ROM the treatment which our Lord received after his first preaching in Nazareth, recorded in the fourth chapter of St. Luke, we should hardly have supposed

that he would so soon have gone thither again. But no doubt his heart was specially drawn toward those who had been his townsmen for so many years, and whom he knew in all the intimacies of social life; and he yearned for their salvation. Hence he was willing to make another effort to disciple them to his faith. This was in accordance with his conduct on a later occasion, when his disciples would dissuade him from going into Judea again by saying, "Master, the Jews of late sought to kill thee, and goest thou thither again?" he heeded not the supposed danger, and went where duty called.

Having, then, waited a sufficient time after his first repulse at Nazareth, for reflection to have sobered their minds, and for rumor to have borne to their ears the wonderful things which he had done in all the region of Galilee, he now bends his steps thither.

The day before he took this journey had witnessed some of his mightiest works. He had crossed the Sea of Galilee to the country of the Gadarenes on the eastern side, and there had cast out "the legion of devils" from him who was possessed, and who, in consequence, dwelt in tombs, and by his fierceness and strength had become the terror of the whole country. This legion of devils Jesus had not only cast out, but permitted, at their own request, to go into a herd of swine two thousand in number, which, contrary to Jewish law, were kept in the vicinity, "and the whole herd ran violently down a steep place into the sea and were choked in the sea." Returning to Capernaum, he was there met by Jairus, the ruler of the Synagogue, with the touching appeal, "My little daughter lieth at the point of death. I pray thee come and lay thy hands on her that she may be healed and she shall live." Not only did he comply, and raise her from the dead (for the servant of the ruler announced to the agonized father before he reached the house, "Thy daughter is dead; trouble not the master"), but on the way to the house of Jairus he healed also, through the virtue that pervaded his very dress, the woman with an issue of blood twelve years, who with great faith, but modest secresy, had come behind and touched the hem of his garment in the assured conviction, "If I may but touch his clothes, I shall be whole."

After a day full of such deeds of divine mercy he ascends the steep hillsides of Tiberias, moves across the plain of Galilee, toils up the rugged hills that shut in Nazareth on the north, and from their summit looks down once more on his childhood's home. In this journey his disciples are with him. He returns to Nazareth not alone, but with the twelve companions and witnesses of his word and works. He goes there also preheralded by the mighty works which he had done elsewhere—works which rumor bore to all ears, but which rumor could not magnify because they already exceeded human imagination.

He went there a few days, doubtless, before the Sabbath, as if to show that he harbored no malice against those who would have cast him down from the brow of the hill on which the city was built, and that, despite their ill-treatment, he still sought their salvation. "When the Sabbath was come," he went, as had been his custom from childhood, to the Synagogue and "began to teach." It was the same Synagogue out of which he had been hustled a few months before, and before the same congregation which had been "filled with wrath" at his first discourse.

There is no intimation here of what he taught,

as there was before, but we know that wherever he went he was "teaching and preaching the gospel of the kingdom."

The effect of it is, however, noted. It produced first astonishment, then distrustful questionings, then offence. Astonishment, or that confusion of mind under the blended influence of wonder and fear at some unexpected appearance or event, was often produced in the minds of his hearers by the strong, bold, true, life-giving words of Jesus.

Though the people of Nazareth had heard him before, yet they listened again with new astonishment. Their minds seemed to be perplexed at such a phenomenon. They wonder how it could be that He who had lived nearly all his life among them, receiving no higher advantages than they, reading no more learned books than they, taught in no school beyond that of the village rabbi, and brought up to the trade of a carpenter, should suddenly appear so wise, so wonderful, so influential, as to fill all Galilee and Judea with the rumor of his words and deeds. "Whence," they ask, "hath this man this wisdom?" They acknowledged the wisdom, but wanted to know "whence it was," and how is it that "such mighty works are wrought by his hands?" Here again the mighty works are acknowledged, but they cannot solve their origin. They thus give unconscious testimony to both, while yet they seek to bring both into discredit by asking, "Is not this the carpenter?" "Is not this the carpenter's son?" "Is not his mother called Mary?" Is he not "the brother of James and Joses, and of Juda and Simon? and his sisters, are they not all with us?" "Whence hath this man these things?"

From these carping questions we learn incidentally several things: that Jesus was not only the reputed son of a carpenter, but was himself a carpenter—learned the trade as a youth and wrought at it as a man; that his reputed father, Joseph, was dead, as no mention is made of him in these questions; that our Lord had brothers and sisters, four being named of the former and several of the latter, whose names are not given; that the family of Mary, the mother of Jesus, was still living at Nazareth, and was one well and reputably known to all the people.

It is not necessary to discuss the question whether the brothers and sisters spoken of here were the children of Joseph and Mary, or the children of Joseph by a former wife, or whether they were merely, as the usage of language would warrant us in believing, the cousins of our Lord, the children of Cleopas or Alpheus. This is a question about which much has been written, concerning which little is known and where conjecture is fruitless. In whatever sense they were related to Mary, they evidently constituted her family, and among the people they passed as the brothers and sisters of our Lord, and this without any rebuke or explanation from Jesus or his disciples.

St. John mentions that the people of Capernaum asked on one occasion nearly the same question as the people of Nazareth: "Is not this Jesus, the son of Joseph, whose father and mother we know? How is it then that he saith, I came down from heaven?"

To these questionings our Lord simply replied, "A prophet is not without honor save in his own country and among his own kin and in his own house." The tenor of the objections, veiled under the questions which they asked among themselves, was that of depreciating his character and works by referring to the lowness of his origin and the humbleness of his occupation and the scantiness of his learning. They thus sought to take away from the force of his teaching and the greatness of his miracles, because they could not comprehend the wisdom or the mighty works which he showed forth.

The reply of our Lord was evidently proverbial. It is one of those truths which have passed into the current thought of all languages, losing nothing of its truth as it flows from age to age and nation to nation.

Every day illustrates the accuracy of this proverb. Few great men can bear the close inspection of social and domestic life. There is a certain perspective point from which you have to look at greatness. If too near, it reveals minute defects—if too distant, you lose some of the finer lineaments; and so a just mean is required between the microscopic, that would dwell on the details, and the telescopic, which notes only large outlines, in order to get a just estimate of real excellence. The treatment which the ancient prophets received from those of their own kin and nation fully illustrates the truth of the sentiment of our Lord. Secular history confirms what Jesus so broadly asserts.

St. Mark says that "they were offended at him" —*i. e.*, scandalized at him. He became to them a subject of gossip and tattle and misrepresentation and contumely. He was talked against and misrepresented and traduced. His words were twisted into wrong meanings. His wondrous miracles were distorted into the working out of evil agencies. This is always the aim of the evil one, a purpose known to our Lord and against which he warned his followers when, after bidding the disciples of John to go and show him what things they had seen and heard, he adds the significant words, "And blessed is he whosoever shall not be offended in me."

It was prophesied (Isa. viii. 14, 15) that Messiah would "be for a stone of stumbling and a rock of offence," that which would be a scandal and a tripping to those who were so blinded by worldliness and self-righteousness that they could not or would not see this "tried stone," this "precious corner-stone," which God laid in Zion for a foundation. What St. Paul calls "the offence of the cross" still exists, and it will continue so long as there is an unrenewed heart on earth, for the same apostle gives us the true reason of it when he says, "The natural mind is enmity against God; it is not subject to the law of God, neither indeed can be." Blessed indeed are those whose eyes have been opened to see the preciousness of that Corner-stone at which the ungodly stumble, and to embrace with loving hearts Him who is to the Jew a stumbling-block and to the Greek foolishness, "but to them that are called, both Jew and Greek, Christ, the wisdom of God and the power of God."

The result of this offence toward Jesus, and unbelief in him, was a depriving them of many temporal blessings which would doubtless have attended his ministry among them, for St. Matthew says, "He did not many mighty works there because of their unbelief." St. Mark uses language which implies an inability to do mighty works resulting from lack of faith in the people: "He could there do no mighty works," etc. It is to be observed here that nearly all the manifestations of the miraculous power of Jesus were made at the solicitation of others, and as an indication of their belief in his ability to do as they desired. It was the response of Jesus to their faith in him. "Believest thou that I am able to do this?" was his question to one. "If thou canst believe, all things are possible to him that believeth," was his rejoinder to another. According to your faith be it unto you, were the terms of his healing grants to others. "O woman, great is thy faith; be it unto thee even as thou wilt," is his language to her whose persistent entreaty told her persisting faith. If the blessings which he had so lavishingly bestowed were desired, they were worth asking for, and in the absence of the faith of the Nazarethites we see the almost total absence of his mighty works. Yet even in that city he left not himself without witness, for he did "lay his hands upon a few sick folk and healed them." There were a few who believed even in the midst of unbelief, and to these sick ones the compassionate Jesus went and laid his holy hands on them. Their faith was rewarded with health, and thus he left a testimony behind him of his mingled compassion and power.

Even these miracles made, it seems, but slight impression, for St. Mark immediately adds, "And he marveled because of their unbelief." In the case of the Centurion of Capernaum whose servant he healed, it is said by St. Matthew that "he marveled" at the greatness of his faith; here we learn "he marveled" at the want of faith in the people of Nazareth.

The Centurion was a Roman, had only heard of Jesus or seen a few of his works, and yet had such faith in him that he did not deem it necessary for Jesus to go to his house to heal his sick servant, but only to give an order to the palsy to go, as he, a soldier, would give an order unto a soldier under him to go, and the palsy, like the soldier, would do the bidding of the Master's word. It was a faith that invested our Lord with the whole command of life and death, and hence he "said to them that followed, Verily I say unto you, I have not found so great faith, no, not in Israel."

The people of Nazareth, however, had seen him, known him, heard him. There was no excuse for their not believing in him save the social jealousies which would not concede the possibility of greatness to one on a social level with themselves, and who could receive their homage only at the cost of their self-disparagement. Hence in this case the wonder of Jesus was excited at their allowing so small an obstacle to hinder their recognition of his mighty works, and for the sake, perhaps, of personal or family pride, refuse to acknowledge the claims of the Son of Mary. It should be stated here, also, that St. John tells us (vii. 5), "Neither did his brethren believe in him"—*i.e.*, did not at that time (though they did afterward, Acts i. 14), accept him as the Messiah, did not give full credence to his claims and become his active disciples. This declaration gives deeper intensity to the meaning of the proverb, "A prophet is not without honor but in his own country and among his own kin and in his own house." Not unfrequently the nearest relatives throw more obstacles in the way of God's children than strangers.

That hardness of heart which could not be penetrated either by the gracious words or the mighty deeds of Jesus might well excite his wonder. It shows, however, that persons may live in the house with Jesus, be his kinsmen according to the flesh, work with him at the same trade, dwell with him many years, worship together Sabbath after Sabbath in the same Synagogue, blend in the intimacies of domestic and social ties, and yet not believe on him. How often have men said, "Oh, if I had only lived in Christ's day and seen his miracles and heard his preaching, I certainly would have been his disciple!" Yet the probabilities are that you would not. The adage, "Familiarity breeds contempt," would have been as active in its workings in your minds as in the minds of the citizens of Nazareth. The heart is fertile in finding excuses for not believing, and, left to itself, seeks darkness rather than light, because its deeds are evil.

The fact is, that we at the present day are in a better attitude for receiving the truth as it is in Jesus than those were who saw and heard and dwelled with him when on earth. To us he is taken out of the common family, social, national surroundings in which he appeared to the Jews. He is lifted above all the extraneous influences which at that time warped and prejudiced the minds of those around him. He is no longer to us the Son of the widow Mary, the brother of James and Joses and Simon and Judas, the carpenter of Nazareth, the peasant of Galilee. To us he no longer wears the ordinary dress of men, followed about from place to place by a retinue of plain fishermen and publicans. To us he does not stand out as the opponent of the scribes and the Pharisees, the rich and the powerful classes, withering them by his woes and exposing their hypocrisies, and receiving in return their poured-out wrath, waxing greater and fiercer until it compasses his death. The sharp outlines of these passing events, stirring to their depths all Syria, commented on from Dan to Beersheba, bruited about with maledictions by scribe and Pharisee, have, with their deteriorating effect on the then acceptance of his person and mission, all passed away; and that which then lessened the proportions of his character, because it was viewed only in a partial light, now augments its greatness, when we see it in its true position and magnitude and under its fully-developed glory.

We are therefore far better off in our real knowledge of Jesus than the people of Nazareth, or than even his brethren were. We have all the testimony which they had, and manifold more. We have the culminating records of centuries of the practical effect of his life and work. We have his atonement as unfolded in the types of Leviticus and as practically at work in reconciling the world unto God. We have his Messiahship as depicted in the glowing words of the old Jewish seers, and as testified to by the wonders of his life and the marvels of his kingdom.

We have his doctrines, not as he dropped his gracious words here and there in the Synagogue, on the mountain-top, by the seashore, at the table, but gathered up in one repository, by holy men writing as they were moved by the Holy Ghost, working out their silent but regenerating effect upon cities, nations and the world.

The thousands of hearts in every age which have drunk in the water of life as it flowed from him, testify that he is precious. The thousands of minds which have bent with intense study upon all the points of his character and his teaching, testify this is the Christ. The thousands of churches, with their ministry and sacraments throughout the world, testify this is the Saviour of men.

Painting, and Sculpture, and Architecture, and Music, and Poetry, and History, and Jurisprudence, and Literature, and Science, in all their higher and truer developments, each pays tribute by their noblest works to "Him in whom are hid all the treasures of wisdom and knowledge." Thus, wherever we look over Christendom, we see proofs of Christ's greatness and glory. From him, as from the world's centre, have gone out the elevating, refining, enlightening, humanizing forces which have driven back ignorance, oppression, and heathenism, with their foul and trooping evils. From him, as from the world's centre, has shot out "the light of the knowledge of the glory of God in the face of Jesus Christ," which is the true light of the mind and heart of men.

And here I cannot but quote the words of one (Theodore Parker) who, having put the life and teachings of Jesus into the crucible of his own free-thinking philosophy, and having subjected them to the test and force of a scorching criticism, finds yet this residuum, which he thus eloquently describes: "How vast has the influence of Jesus been! How it has wrought in the world! His words judge the nations. The wisest son of man has not measured their height. They speak to what is deepest in profound men; to what is holiest in good men; to what is divinest in religious men. They kindle anew the flame of devotion in hearts long cold. They are spirit and life. His truth was not derived from Moses and Solomon; but the light of God shone through him, not colored nor bent aside. His life is the perpetual rebuke of all time since. It condemns ancient civilization; it condemns modern civilization. Wise men we have since had, and good men, but this Galilean youth strode before the world whole thousands of years, so much of divinity was in him. His words solve the questions of this present age. . . . . Let men improve never so far in civilization, or soar never so high on the wings of religion and love, they can never outgo the flight of truth and Christianity. It will always be above them. It is as if we were to fly toward a star, which becomes the larger and more bright the nearer we approach, till we enter and are absorbed in its glory."

If, therefore, Jesus marveled at the unbelief of those around him then, may he not, does he not, wonder still more at your unbelief, with your great light and knowledge? You do not enough think how many more reasons to believe in Christ press upon us in the nineteenth century than existed in the first. How the weight of evidence is rolling itself up more and more with each advancing age! Standing, then, before the Bible, with all the light of eighteen hundred years of Christian hope and achievement thrown upon its sacred pages, how can you resist its claims, reject its enshrined Christ, and remain an unbeliever? A great responsibility is thus laid upon all who dwell in Christian lands, and under the influences of the Church of God. The possession of a Bible lifts you up into a degree of moral accountability before God truly astounding. For in that Bible you find an offered Saviour and a free salvation. Reject it, disuse it, and you cannot be saved, for Jesus only is "the way, the truth, the life." Accept it, use it prayerfully, believe it fully, and it will lead you to the cross here, and to a crown hereafter.

CHAPTER XI.

THE HEALING OF THE BLIND MAN ON THE SABBATH.

"And as Jesus passed by, he saw a man which was blind from his birth. And his disciples asked him, saying, Master, who did this sin, this man, or his parents, that he was born blind? Jesus answered, Neither hath this man sinned, nor his parents: but that the works of God should be made manifest in him. I must work the works of him that sent me, while it is day: the night cometh, when no man can work. As long as I am in the world, I am the light of the world. When he had thus spoken he spat on the ground, and made clay of the spittle, and he anointed the eyes of the blind man with the clay, and said unto him, Go, wash in the pool of Siloam (which is by interpretation, Sent). He went his way, therefore, and washed, and came seeing. The neighbors therefore, and they which before had seen him that he was blind, said, Is not this he that sat and begged? Some said, This is he: others said, He is like him: but he said, I am he. Therefore said they unto him, How were thine eyes opened? He answered and said, A man that is called Jesus, made clay, and anointed mine eyes, and said unto me, Go to the pool of Siloam, and wash: and I went and washed, and I received sight. Then said they unto him, Where is he? He said, I know not. They brought to the Pharisees him that aforetime was blind. And it was the sabbath-day when Jesus made the clay, and opened his eyes. Then again the Pharisees also asked him how he had received his sight. He said unto them, He put clay upon mine eyes, and I washed, and do see. Therefore said some of the Pharisees, This man is not of God, because he keepeth not the sabbath-day. Others said, How can a man that is a sinner do such miracles? And there was a division among them. They say unto the blind man again, What sayest thou of him, that he hath opened thine eyes? He said, He is a prophet. But the Jews did not believe concerning him, that he had been blind, and received his sight, until they

SILOAM.

called the parents of him that had received his sight. And they asked them, saying, Is this your son, who ye say was born blind? How then doth he now see? His parents answered them and said, We know that this is our son, and that he was born blind: but by what means he now seeth, we know not; or who hath opened his eyes, we know not: he is of age; ask him: he shall speak for himself. These words spake his parents, because they feared the Jews: for the Jews had agreed already, that if any man did confess that he was Christ, he should be put out of the Synagogue. Therefore said his parents, He is of age; ask him. Then again called they the man that was blind, and said unto him, Give God the praise: we know that this man is a sinner. He answered and said, Whether he be a sinner or no, I know not: one thing I know, that, whereas I was blind, now I see. Then said they to him again, What did he to thee? how opened he thine eyes? He answered them, I have told you already, and ye did not hear; wherefore would ye hear it again? will ye also be his disciples? Then they reviled him, and said, Thou art his disciple; but we are Moses' disciples. We know that God spake unto Moses; as for this fellow, we know not from whence he is. The man answered and said unto them, Why, herein is a marvelous thing, that ye know not from whence he is, and yet he hath opened mine eyes. Now we know that God heareth not sinners: but if any man be a worshiper of God, and doeth his will, him he heareth. Since the world began was it not heard that any man opened the eyes of one that was born blind. If this man were not of God, he could do nothing. They answered and said unto him, Thou wast altogether born in sins, and dost thou teach us? And they cast him out. Jesus heard that they had cast him out: and when he had found him, he said unto him, Dost thou believe on the Son of God? He answered and said, Who is he, Lord, that I might believe on him? And Jesus said unto him, Thou hast both seen him, and it is he that talketh with thee. And he said, Lord, I believe. And he worshiped him. JOHN ix. 1-38.

HESE passages bring before us the transactions and words of Jesus on the Sabbath after the Feast of Tabernacles, in or near the temple.

The man whose case is here recorded was probably one of that class of beggars who were accustomed to frequent the gates of the temple, that they might do as the lame man healed by Peter and John did, "ask alms of them that entered into the temple."

The cry of the man for help, coupled perhaps with his own sad plight, arrested the attention of the disciples, and prompted it may be by what our Lord not long before had said to the impotent man, when he found him in the temple, "sin no more, lest a worse thing come upon thee," they were induced to ask the question, " Master, who did sin, this man or his parents, that he was born blind?" The connection of sin with disease was a doctrine well known to the Jews, and had been taught to them by type and precept for many hundred years. They were made to feel that sin, disobedience to God's law, brought upon man its sore temporal chastenings, and that the evils thus visited upon themselves for their transgressions were transmitted to their children and children's children.

This biblical truth had, however, been much perverted, and had given rise to fanciful theories by which to account for the presence of sickness and calamities of various kinds. The question of the disciples brings out two forms of this false theory: first, that the congenital blindness of the man might be the result of sin on the part of "his parents" before he was born, thus visiting directly and personally the sin of the father upon the child. Second, that the blindness of the man now might perhaps have been caused by some sin of his in a former state of being. For though the Jews generally did not believe in the pre-existence or transmigration of souls, yet the Essenes and Cabalists did hold these views, and by them interpreted and accounted for the evils of this present being. To this question of the disciples our Lord at once replies, "Neither did this man sin, nor his parents." Not that they were not sinners, "for there is no man that liveth and sinneth not," but that they were not sinners in the sense which their question implied, as drawing down upon themselves as parents, or upon this man as their son, this specific evil for some supposed specific sin before he was born. The man was not born blind for any offence committed either by himself or his parents. Thus that whole class of ideas which cropped out in this question, and which evidently had found entrance into the disciples' minds, was swept away by a single sentence.

This negation of the question was made stronger by an affirmation which declared that the blindness of the man was a result of God's providential ordering, "that the works of God should be made manifest in him," the idea doubtless being that this blindness would be overruled by God for the showing forth of his glory in his restoration to sight. Thus the physical and temporal evil would be transmuted into a spiritual and eternal blessing, not to the man only, but, through the record of his cure, to the whole world. Recognizing in this blind man a condition of things in the relief of which he could manifest a work of God, Jesus said, as if addressing those who would dissuade him (in consequence of the Jews having just before taken up stones to stone him) from doing any further act of mercy on the Sabbath, "I must work the work of Him that sent me while it is day: the night cometh in which no man can work." In speaking of himself as being "sent" into the world, he speaks in reference to that voluntary subordination of himself as Mediator and Redeemer, which he made when He "who was in the form of God thought it not robbery to be equal with God, but made himself of no reputation and took upon him the form of a servant and was made in the likeness of men." That self-humiliation which he manifested when he said, as is recorded by the Psalmist (xl. 6) and St. Paul (Heb. x. 7), "Lo, I come to do thy will, O God; yea, thy law is within my heart."

"The works" of God which he was thus "sent" to do, were those works of grace, mercy, truth, which were so fully illustrated in the gracious words which proceeded out of his mouth, in the many mighty works of healing mercy, and in the enunciation of those divine truths, the concrete of which he himself summed up in the one grand declaration, "I am the way, the truth, the life." His wondrous miracles did this, and accredited him as one "sent from God," even as Nicodemus reasons, "for no man can do the works that thou doest except God be with him."

But Christ's spiritual work was to have, as it were, its parallel physical work running alongside of the spiritual, and attesting and authenticating at every step his divinity, headship and power. Our Lord gave a synopsis of this work in the text of his first sermon in the Synagogue of Nazareth, where, quoting from Isaiah, he said,

"The Spirit of the Lord is upon me, because he hath anointed me to preach the gospel to the poor; he hath sent me to heal the broken-hearted, to preach deliverance to the captives and recovering of sight to the blind, to set at liberty them that are bruised, to preach the acceptable year of the Lord;" and he announced himself as doing this work when he said, "This day is this Scripture fulfilled in your ears." Christ's working day was then drawing to a close. But a few months intervened between him and the cross, when the night of death would put an end to his earthly work, for before he died on that cross he uttered words which showed that his work was done, as he cried, "It is finished!" and "gave up the ghost." This allusion to his life-work as a "day" is several times made by him, and in reference to his labors therein he declares, "My meat is to do the will of Him that sent me and to finish his work."

Having thus spoken of the necessity of working "while it is day," he then makes the sublime assertion, "As long as I am in the world I am the light of the world." It was prophesied of the Messiah that he should "open the blind eyes, bring out the prisoners from the prison, and them that sit in darkness out of the prison house." Isa. xlii. 7, 8. It was declared in reference to him that "the people that walked in darkness have seen a great light: they that dwell in the land of the shadow of death, upon them hath the light shined;" and the same prophet, casting his vision across the ages, calls out to Israel, in view of the advent of Jesus, "Arise, shine, for thy light is come, and the glory of the Lord is risen upon thee! Gentiles shall come to thy light, and kings to the brightness of thy rising."

He was announced also figuratively as "the star out of Jacob," "the day star," "the dayspring from on high," "the sun of righteousness" that should arise "with healing in his wings," or beams. In making the assertion, then, "I am the light of the world," Jesus had gathered up into himself the predictions and symbols of the olden seers, and gave them a personal and corporate form.

On several occasions he applies the term "light" to himself. In his conversation with Nicodemus, and also in those discourses recorded in the 12th chapter of John, when he said, "Yet a little while is the light with you; walk while ye have the light, lest darkness come upon you. While ye have light believe in the light, that ye may be the children of light." And then, that there might be no question as to who or what this light was, he adds, "I am come a light into the world, that whosoever believeth on me should not abide in darkness."

As he stood in the temple on one of the mornings of this Feast of Tabernacles, he said to those around him, "I am the light of the world; he that followeth me shall not walk in darkness, but shall have the light of life." The next day, standing beside the blind man in the temple, he repeats the same declaration, "I am the light of the world," as if he had said, I am in the moral and spiritual firmament what the sun is in the physical firmament, the source and centre of all light. I am the moral and spiritual light of the world.

This must have seemed to those who heard him, and who saw in him little to distinguish him from other men, a very bold, self-assertive, even arrogant claim. When had any of their renowned rabbis, Hillel or Shammai or Gamaliel, ever spoken of themselves in this manner?

When had ever any of the great philosophers of the world, Plato, Socrates, Aristotle, ever put forth such pretensions? and who was this Galilean carpenter that he should make this assertion of claims that could exist only in the Messiah? Accustomed as we are to regard Christ as the light of the world, is it difficult for us to enter into the astonishment of those who heard him first lay claim to be this light of the world, and how their national pride, and their personal prejudices, and their sectarian views, stoutly rose up in resistance of any such Messianic assumptions by this son of a carpenter! Looking back as we can over a space of eighteen hundred years, and interpreting Jesus' words in the light of fulfilled prophecy and a triumphing Christianity, we can see how literally true they were, and that look at him in any and every aspect, he is indeed, as St. John declared he was, "the true light that lighteth every man that cometh into the world."

Take the *revealing* power of light and examine Jesus' character in that phase, and see how well the term applies to him. Light, as we know, reveals or makes manifest things; the opposite of darkness, which covers up and hides them.

Now with all that the human intellect had done in the regions of mind and morals, with all the great philosophical discoveries of the sages and magi in Egypt, in Persia, in Greece, in Rome, there were certain regions into which their speculations had not penetrated, and certain topics which they had in vain labored to comprehend or explain. There was, with all their metaphysical acquisitions, a large *terra incognita* in the region of mind and morals. There were undiscovered continents of man's spiritual relationship lying unknown beyond the *ultima thule* of Seneca's visions, or the half-ventured hopes of Socrates. As to the cause and consequences of man's fall; as to the origin and prevalence of evil; as to the knowledge of the true God, the way to reach him, the way to worship him, his attributes, his manifestations; as to the real object and aim of this present life, with its unsolvable mysteries; as to any future life beyond the grave; as to all the great problems of life and death, good and evil, soul and body, men and angels, future rewards and punishments,— the universal mind was in darkness and needed revelation, light—REVEALING LIGHT. And just here it is that upon each and all these points Christ sheds light.

He reveals to us "the way" to God, "the truth" of God, "the life" of God. He has "brought life and immortality to light in the gospel." He has taught us that "God is a spirit, and must be worshiped in spirit and in truth." He has made known to us the true aims and destinies of our mortal being. He has revealed the grace of God in the salvation of fallen man, through the terms and conditions of repentance and faith, and thus shown us that sin can be conquered, that death can be vanquished, that the grave can be stripped of its victory, so that, in the strong language of the apostle, "the light of the knowledge of the glory of God is revealed to us in the face of Jesus Christ," "who is the brightness of the Father's glory, the express image of his person." He is thus THE REVEALER, the light-dispenser, the scatterer of darkness and doubt, and the bringer-in of a bright and eternal day. From the face of the Sun of righteousness are shot out those widespread and deep-penetrating beams of light which drive away the trooping shadows of superstition and error, and which will eventually fill the earth with "the light of Jesus Christ."

Or, take again the *life-giving* power of light, and see how true it is that Jesus is, in this aspect, "the light of the world."

The researches of modern chemistry prove what experience has for long ages taught men, that there are certain kinds of rays in the beams of the sun which are absolutely necessary to ensure vegetable and animal life and growth. Could these peculiar rays be removed from the sun, though an illuminating quality might remain, its life-giving and sustaining power would be lost, and man, and beast, and bird, and tree, and flower, would wilt and die.

Just so with the light which Jesus sheds. It is not merely enlightening, it is life-giving. This St. John brings out most clearly in the opening chapter of his Gospel. "In him," he says, "was *life*, and the *life* was *the light* of men." The argument is, Christ is the light, but the light of Christ is seen by us finite beings only in his life. That *life* becomes our *light*, our *guide*. It is the lamp in the tall tower of his holy character which reflects that inner light in its outlook over the sea of humanity. It is his own life, the life spiritual, that Jesus imparts to all his followers; and because they seek to imitate him in his shining virtues, they become themselves "children of light," and their light shines before men, that men seeing their good works may glorify their Father which is in heaven. Thus the light of Christ in the soul is always life-giving, life-sustaining and life-developing.

Yet once more, look upon the *beautifying* power of light, and mark how, in this aspect also, Jesus is "the light of the world." All the beautiful coloring of nature, from the gorgeous clouds to the seven-listed rainbow; from the most delicate penciling of the tiniest flower to the broad bands of rosy glory which flash up in the restless northern lights; all the thousand-tinted glories which have been lavished in the painting of field, and forest, and flower, and sky, and sea, and the works of man's device,—all these are due to the beautifying power of light, to the divisibility of its rays, to the different angles of its refraction, to the varying velocities of its ethereal waves as they pulsate from the sun, and to the manifold densities and reflecting or refracting power of the objects on which those rays impinge. So that if the light be taken away, all tint and color is gone, the beautifying power is withheld, and colorless patches and tintless fields, and a dull, unvarying uniformity of darkness, would clothe all nature. And as we look at the moral world, do we not find that all its beauty is derived from Jesus, the light of the world? Sin is deformity, derangement, darkness, death. Sin is error, perversion, untruthfulness, doubt. Sin is foul, polluting, defiling, wrecking alike to soul and body.

Sin defies God, rejects Christ, quenches the Spirit, kills the body and destroys the soul in hell!

What are all the loathsome and vile and abominable scenes in daily life? What are all the great diseases and sores and wounds of our common humanity? What are all the waste places and deserts and wildernesses of poverty and ignorance and superstition? What are all the Stygian lakes of human lusts and bestial crimes? What, we ask, are all these, and everything else that disfigures our once fair earth, but sin's work?

But where the light of Christ shines, there these darksome and doleful things flee away, and beauty, moral beauty, springs up. As the light of Christ shines into the individual heart it decks the heart with unearthly beauty, and a character that grows silently and symmetrically as the palm tree, developing all its beauty out of an inner life "hid with Christ in God," towers up in graceful luxuriance before us, and the world says, What a beautiful character!

As the light of Christ shines into a family, making father, mother, child, brother, sister, luminous with the holy light of truth and purity and love, how the elements of that family harmonize and commingle into exquisite pictures of domestic life under the sweet groupings and the rich colorings of the Holy Ghost! As the light of Christ shines into and permeates society, how it purifies, ennobles and then beautifies it!

It is his light that has vivified and quickened into life all the native excellences of heart and mind, because even what was good in human nature could not develop itself amid the darkness of heathenism, and only comes out under the light of pure religion; and not only so, but by resolving the entire duty of man to man, and man to God, into one great commandment, whose root principle is love, as Jesus did, he has bound society together by this love-tie, which, in its daily effects on the individual character, is gradually expelling all that is contrary to this "first and great commandment," and cementing together heart to heart, and rank to rank, and class to class, and tribe to tribe, until love shall rule all hearts in their dealings one with another, and love pervade all hearts in their actings toward God; and thus love will be "the fulfilling of the law." What a beautiful aspect will a family, a society, a nation, a world, present to the eye human, as well as to the eye divine, when all shall be illuminated by the light of Christ, when all shall seek to walk in that light, and as children of light hold forth, each in the candlestick of his own profession, the word of life as the law of his heart and the hope of his soul!

There were many founders of religion and philosophy who styled themselves, or were styled by others, "the lights of the world." Confucius, who lived five hundred years before Christ and founded the great state religion of China, is mostly represented in Chinese pictures in the attitude of prayer, while a beam of light from heaven descends upon his book of wisdom, out of which he teaches his scholars as they stand admiringly around, showing that the popular idea of the Chinese concerning their highest sage was that of the receiver and imparter of light from heaven.

Zoroaster, who lived about the same century and founded the religion of the Parsees, as developed in the sacred books of the Zendavesta, made light the pure and eternal source of all perfection. He considered himself as belonging to the kingdom of light, and felt called upon to fight with all his strength against the kingdom of darkness; and hence the good principle of his religion, or Ormuzd, is termed the light of the world, which by its working seeks to transform everything to light.

Apollo, the most influential god in the religion of Greece, and concerning whom it has been justly said "that the Greeks would never have become what they were without the worship of Apollo," is always represented as born of light and as being the god of light, and his work, according to the mythology of the day, was to diffuse light in all the regions of mind, and in all the arts and sciences of men. Hence the sun is the emblem of this powerful divinity. Indeed, all the religious systems of the world sought to establish themselves as the light of the world. But they signally failed. Their light did not illumine the hearts of their founders. The brilliancy of their thoughts and the flashes of their yearning spirits, like the shimmer of heat-lightning in the evening, only made the surrounding darkness more dark by contrast with their fitful and unprofitable light.

But it is not so with Jesus, and the religion which he established.

Let us not forget, too, the intense force of the definite article "*the*" here, that Jesus is *the* light of the world. Not *a* light, one among many others and of equal value, and no more, but the article *the*, being *exclusive* as well as *emphatic*, shows that Jesus, and *Jesus only*, is the light of the world. There is no other source and fountain of spiritual light. All comes from him, and other lights, like the planets of the solar system, shine only in his light, and show forth, therefore, only a reflected glory. In saying, " As long as I am in the world I am the light of the world," Jesus did not mean to convey the idea that his light-imparting power was tied to his earthly life, and would cease when that terminated. Far from it; for though he is taken bodily from us, he is still here by his Spirit, by his Word, by his

Sacraments, by his Church, by his Ministers. His assurance to his disciples, and through them to all the spiritual generations of men, was, "Lo, I am with you alway, even to the end of the world," "I will not leave you comfortless (orphans), I will come unto you," "Where two or three are gathered together in my name, there am I in the midst of them."

The meaning, then, is that he would ever be the enlightening power of the world. He would never cease to shine on men as the light of life, the light-giving life and the life-imparting light. In the days of his flesh he shone on only a limited circle; his light was circumscribed; its beams shot into and were almost lost in the thick fogs and haze of Jewish prejudice and hatred and unbelief. Now, however, he is lifted above his earthly surroundings. He is no longer girt around by the hills of Galilee or Judea. He has ascended on high, "gone up with a shout, and our God with the voice of a trump," and from the heaven above, and from before the throne, he still shines out the "light of life," because he is ever "the King of glory."

CHAPTER XII.

THE HEALING OF THE BLIND MAN ON THE SABBATH.

(CONTINUED.)

HAVING thus prepared his auditors by telling them that he was "the light of the world," Jesus proceeds to give them ocular proof of the truth of his assertion by a miracle which would at once illustrate his meaning and demonstrate his power.

"He spat on the ground and made clay of the spittle, and anointed the eyes of the blind man with the clay, and said unto him, Go wash in the pool of Siloam." The question at once arises, Why did our Lord interpose three distinct instrumentalities between himself and the completed miracle, the clay, the spittle, the washing in Siloam? The reply is that at times he chose to work with means, and at times without means, and the reason of his doing so may generally be found in some circumstance connected with the specific case before him. The miracle was not the less a putting forth of divine power, in that he chose to use intermediaries which of themselves, and without the divine power operating through them, were yet powerless to heal. The use of these media was in accommodation to the request of those asking the miracle, or to the weak faith of the patient. Jesus needed them not. He could heal at a distance and without seeing the object of his miraculous cure, as he did the nobleman's son (John iv. 46–53) and the centurion's servant. Luke vii. 1–10. He could heal with a word, without a touch, as he did the ten lepers (Luke xvii. 11–19) and the two blind men near Jericho. Matt. xx. 29–34. He could heal without a word, or a conscious touch on his part, as in the case of the woman having an issue of blood. Matt. ix. 20–22. He could heal with a touch and a word, as in the case of Peter's wife's mother (Matt. viii. 14–17) and the woman with a spirit of infirmity eighteen years. Luke xiii. 11–13.

We find two other cases in the New Testament somewhat analogous to the one under consideration. One was as he was passing through the coast of Decapolis, where "they bring unto him one that was deaf and had an impediment in his speech, and they beseech him to put his hand upon him." Mark vii. 31–37. The other was wrought in the vicinity of Bethsaida, where "they bring a blind man unto him, and they besought him to touch him." Mark viii. 22–26. It will be observed as to both these cases that the men were brought to Jesus, that in each case he was asked to touch them by those who brought them. Hence in each case our Lord accommodated his work of healing to the apprehension of his auditors, and used such interventions as would arrest their attention, while yet their use would take off nothing from the greatness of the miracle. So in the case before us. The man had not asked to be healed, nor had any one asked healing on his behalf. Indeed, it appears that he had perhaps never before heard of Jesus, and hence could have no faith in him. It was necessary, therefore, in such a case, to implant the beginnings of hope and faith in his mind by calling the man to him, and thus raise an expectation in him of some relief; then, having prepared the unguent and anointed his eyes, deepening that expectation into hope; then preparing him for the final blessing by putting his just developing faith into action, and telling him to "go to the pool of Siloam and wash." The call, the anointing, the command, the going, the washing, were so many ascending steps in the development of that man's faith; each was based on the former, and all together rendered easy the ascent from ignorance of Jesus to that full belief in him which he so speedily manifested. The several processes of healing corresponded to the several processes in the blind man's mind, just as they evidently did in the case of the blind man near Bethsaida. The cure lay in neither the clay, the spittle nor the pool, but in the doing of what Jesus told him to do, and while obeying he reaped the blessing.

The pool of Siloam, mentioned as far back as Nehemiah (iii. 15), to which he was sent to wash, still exists, just outside the southern wall of Jerusalem, in the village of Siloam, and is one of the few undisputed localities in that region. It seems to have been connected with the temple mount by a rocky, sinuous conduit which brought to a lower and walled-in basin, called "the pool," the waters that flowed from the spring beneath the temple area above. It is to this that Milton alludes when he speaks of

> "Siloa's brook, that flowed
> "Fast by the oracle of God."

It is now a mere ruin of crumbling walls, broken columns, decaying steps. The water itself is brackish and unclean, the place is dank and filthy, and the whole surroundings are as unromantic in fact as Milton has made it romantic in song.

Jesus, having anointed the eyes of this man with the clay, told him to go and wash in Siloam, but did not tell him what would result therefrom. "He went his way therefore and washed, and came seeing." The result was not only sight to the eyes of the body, but to the eyes of the soul, for he saw at one and the same time the light of day—the sun; and the light of the world—Jesus; and at once, in the presence of Pharisees and doubters, he acknowledged his cure as a miracle done by a prophet come from God. Now follows a most interesting and lifelike dialogue, first with his neighbors, then with the Pharisees, then with Jesus. It is related by St. John with all the vividness of an eye-witness and with the graphic pen of a word-painter, setting before us the ensuing events with picturesque beauty and fidelity.

We judge from the narrative that immediately on his regaining his sight the man went to his home, as the first attestants to the reality of his cure are his "neighbors." They "which before had seen him that he was blind, said, Is not this he that sat and begged?" They saw a change so great in the whole aspect of the man, that some could scarcely say whether it were he or not. In this variance of opinions they resort to the blind man himself, and he promptly tells them, "I am he." At once they ask, "How were thine eyes opened?" He answers, "A man that is called Jesus made clay and anointed mine eyes, and said unto me, Go to the pool of Siloam and wash, and I went and washed and received sight." This is clear and succinct, and yet it implies that the man probably had never heard of Jesus before that day, and knew perhaps nothing of his character and fame. The neighbors immediately inquire where Jesus is, but the man can only reply, "I know not."

Unwilling to let the matter rest here, the

once blind man was brought before the Pharisees—*i. e.*, to the lesser Sanhedrim. This body consisted of twenty-three members in every city in Palestine in which there were not less than one hundred and twenty householders, and its office was to determine minor cases of civil and ecclesiastical law, carrying up to the greater Sanhedrim of seventy-one members, as to a court of appeal, the weightier cases beyond the province of the lesser Sanhedrim. Before this tribunal this once blind man is brought, not so much, as it would seem, to punish him for anything done on the Sabbath day, as to get his testimony to what Jesus did, that they might have whereof to accuse him of Sabbath-breaking.

Standing before this judicial body, he gives to their query "how he had received his sight" (for the fact itself was never disputed) nearly the same answer as to his neighbors. This answer produced a division in the council. One party, looking at it only in its bearing on the Sabbatic law, said, "This man is not of God, because he keepeth not the Sabbath day;" while another party, looking at it from its miraculous side, argued, "How can a man that is a sinner do such miracles?"

Unable to reach any unanimity, they turn to the man standing in their midst and ask him how he regards the person who wrought this cure. At once, without a moment's hesitation, he replies, "He is a prophet." His process of reasoning seems to be not unlike that of Nicodemus, who said, "We know that thou art a teacher come from God, for no man can do these miracles that thou doest except God be with him"—a sound conclusion from right premises. This confession of the man, however, did not satisfy them, and so they tried another device. They rejected the story that the man had been blind and had received his sight, thus virtually making Jesus and the blind man conspire together to impose a false miracle on the people. Hence they summon before them the parents of the man, in the hope that they may perhaps secure from them such a confession as will enable them to proclaim the whole transaction fraudulent. To the question of the tribunal, "Is this your son?" the parents promptly reply, "We know that this is our son." To the question, Do ye say he was born blind? they as explicitly answer, "He was born blind;" and to the last question, "How then doth he now see?"

they could only say, whether from ignorance or fear, "By what means he now seeth we know not, or who hath opened his eyes we know not; he is of age, ask him; he shall speak for himself." The testimony that he was born blind is now conclusive. Yet how completely did his parents truckle to their fears of being excommunicated, in the thoroughly evasive, if not absolutely false, answer as to the person by whom their son had been healed! They knew that it was Jesus, for their son had told them so; they knew the method by which it was done, for that also had been told them. But the hostile party to Jesus in the council had already agreed to "cast out of the Synagogue" any that should confess that Jesus was the Christ; and knowing this, they evaded any such confession by throwing the burden of proving the miracle upon their son, who was of age and who could speak for himself.

Failing here to get any evidence of collusion or deceit, they recall the son; and addressing him with apparently devout, yet really hypocritical, words, and uttered in a manner as if to convey to him the idea, Well, we have found out the trick and have adjudged this Jesus a sinner, and you must therefore side with us and conform to our views, they say, "Give God the praise, we know that this man is a sinner." The direction "Give God the praise" does not mean, as at first sight it might appear, as a call upon the healed man to return thanks to God for his cure, for they could not thus ask him to acknowledge the cure as being worthy of praise to God, while yet he who wrought it was "a sinner." We must put the two parts of the sentence together, and interpret one by the other. Hence we infer that the idea in the minds of the Jews in uttering it was to adjure him to speak the truth, just as Joshua (vii. 19) adjured Achan, who by his deeds had brought such disaster upon Israel, saying, "My son, give, I pray thee, glory to the Lord God of Israel, and make confession unto him, and tell me now what thou hast done: hide it not from me."

By this solemn adjuration, coupled with their solemn judgment, this "man is a sinner," they hoped to overawe the man, and extort out of him some confession that will break down the force of the miracle and destroy its popular effects. But they signally failed. The man answered, "Whether he be a sinner or no I know not," it is not my province to enter upon that question, but "one thing I know, that whereas I was blind, now I see." The Jews now resort to a kind of cross-examination, to elicit if possible some discrepancy in his testimony on which to invalidate it altogether; hence they ask him again to go over the matter with them. He ill brooks this questioning, and replies with tartness and irony, "I have told ye already, and ye did not hear; wherefore would ye hear it again: will ye also be his disciples?" By telling them "ye did not hear" he meant that they did not credit his testimony, hence it was useless to ask again; and by the question, "Will ye also be his disciples?" he doubtless meant to insinuate that all their seeming anxiety to sift the facts of this miracle was not because of their desire to learn the real truth, and thus, if it proved Jesus to be the Christ, to enrol themselves as his disciples, but was solely prompted by a hatred of him which had already formulated itself into a resolve to cast out of the Synagogue any who should become Jesus' disciple. This reply drew forth their indignation; and reviling him with opprobrious epithets, they drew the line of distinction between him

CASTING THE BLIND MAN OUT OF THE SYNAGOGUE.

and them, saying, "Thou art his disciple, but we are Moses' disciples; we know that God spake unto Moses, but as to this fellow, we know not whence he is."

The cogency of the man's reply they could not resist, while yet it not only failed to convince their minds, but stimulated them to such rage that they turned upon him in indignation, saying, "Thou wast altogether born in sin, and dost thou teach us?" Their rage culminated in their casting him out—*i. e.*, not only turned him with violence out of the judgment-hall, where this discussion took place, but also excommunicated him from the Synagogue. This was as far as they could judicially go—a deprivation of certain religious privileges coupled with formal maledictions and popular reproach.

Some one immediately informed Jesus of the result of this trial, and he at once sought the man and "found him." It was for Jesus' sake that he had been cast out, and he never permits a man to suffer for him without the comfort of his presence and support. "The good Shepherd seeks the poor sheep cast out by the wicked ones; the Son of God will reveal himself to him who for his name's sake is reviled and evil-entreated of men;" and he rejoices against the whole host of the Pharisees over this one mendicant soul whom he has won. He was now to experience the truth of what Jesus had said in his sermon on the mount: "Blessed are ye when men shall revile you and persecute you, and shall say all manner of evil against you falsely for my sake; rejoice, and be exceeding glad, for great shall be your reward in heaven, for so persecuted they the prophets which were before you." He who spoke this eighth beatitude was now to prove its truth by going at once to this persecuted and cast-out man that he may bring him wholly to himself as a full disciple. His first question to him when he finds him is designed to sound the depth of his faith—to make the man reveal (not to Jesus, for he knows what is in man) to his own consciousness the amount of his knowledge of Jesus, and hence he asks, "Dost thou believe on the Son of God?" In this question is folded up the whole doctrine of the Messiah, of the atonement, of the salvation of mankind; for as we learn afterwards in the teaching of our Lord's apostles, to believe on the Son of God is to embrace all the doctrine of Jesus brought to light in the gospel.

This man evidently understood by the term "Son of God" the promised Messiah, and his mind, softened by the influences already at work, was in a state of preparation to believe when one sufficiently accredited should claim that belief. Hence he appeals to Jesus, and says, "Who is he, Lord, that I might believe on him?"

And now He who revealed light into his bodily eye reveals himself unto the soul of this seeker after God as "the light to lighten the Gentiles of the glory of God's people Israel," for without any paraphrasis he directly unfolds himself to his receptive mind, and tells him, "Thou hast both seen him, and it is he that talketh with thee." This is a clear, explicit, straightforward declaration of his Messiahship—as clear as that made to the woman of Samaria, and like her this once blind man accepted it as true. Faith immediately sprung up in his soul; he made his lips confess it, saying, "Lord, I believe," and he carried out his subjective faith to an objective act, for he "worshiped him."

Receiving this divine worship as justly his due, Jesus said to the Pharisees and others who had gathered around him, "For judgment I am come into this world, that they which see not might see, and that they which see might be made blind." These are strange and almost paradoxical words, yet they are full of the deepest and most important truth. On reading them the question immediately arises, How can this be reconciled with those passages in which our Lord asserts just the contrary words? In conversing with Nicodemus, he said, "God sent not his Son into the world to condemn the world," and just before his death he declared, "If any man hear my words and believe not, I judge him not; for I came not to judge the world, but to save the world." John xii. 47. These assertions seem to be diametrically opposite, but it is only a *seeming* contradiction, not a real one. Both statements are true, and the difference which appears on their face vanishes when we get beneath the surface and go down to the real meaning of the words employed. Jesus Christ did not come to this earth for the purpose of executing the office of a judge of men. Hence, when one dissatisfied with the distribution of a father's estate came to him with complaints, and said, "Master, speak to my brother that he divide the inheritance with me," Jesus replied, "Man, who made me a judge or a divider over you?" So also when the scribes and Pharisees brought to him "a women taken in adultery," and having stated to him the Mosaic penalty of such an act, asked him, "But what sayest thou?" he declined to act as judge. He knew that they wished to entrap him into a judicial decision; and if he had given his opinion for or against the woman, they would in either case have accused him of usurping a power which did not belong to him, and for the exercise of which they would have condemned him. It was not his business to pronounce upon her guilt or innocence. He was not there to act as a judge in such cases, and hence he met their question by the reply, "Let him that is without sin first cast a stone at her." In this sense, then, as occupying a judicial station, our Lord did not come to judge the world.

But there is another kind of judgment than forensic or judicial—a judgment which results as an effect from the manifestation of certain principles or doctrines; a judgment which is ever working itself out in the development of human character under the presence and teaching of certain great truths. For example, take a garment which is full of stains and imperfections, both of fabric and color, but which are invisible by the light of a candle or in the twilight, and bring it under a mid-day sun, and you at once judge and condemn the garment as unworthy by the simple fact that you expose its defects by an increase of light.

Introduce a great scientific truth into the world, like that, for example, of the Copernican system in astronomy, and its very existence and demonstration judges and condemns all previous and later theories, from the world-centred system of Ptolemy to the vortices of Descartes; for the very demonstration and reception of a great truth, condemns and judges all so-called truths which militate with it.

Thus it was that the very manifestation of Christ in the flesh did, without any formal sentence, condemn the false religions, the false philosophies and the false ethics of the world.

He came as revealing the one living and true God, existing as a spirit, and to be worshiped as a spirit "in spirit and in truth;" and that great thought will, in its workings, overturn every idol god, every priesthood of sin, every temple of error, every religion of man's device.

He came as "the way, the truth, the life," the very point about which all the philosophy of the world had busied itself, and concerning which all had erred; for while to find a *way* to God, to get at the *truth* of God and to obtain a *life* with God was the one aim of all philosophical inquiry, not one could say, I have found it, but each seemed in error's wandering maze to be irretrievably lost.

The centring of them all in Christ, and the manifesting them fully in him, was a virtual condemnation of all human philosophy in just so far as that philosophy was at variance with divine truth.

The bringing in of true godliness showed what was false. The manifestation of incarnate truth, virtually condemned all human error, and the incarnation of the true God, detected as with Ithuriel's spear, the falsities of pagan worship, and made the dark and miserable rites of heathenism start up discovered and amazed, and "return perforce to their own likeness." Whatever, then, is a test of character, or elicits men's views of themselves, or discerns between good and evil, and causes men to show what their real disposition is, is a virtual judgment upon men, and these processes of judgment are continually going on in our minds and continually witnessed in daily life, where there can be of course no judicial sentence or formal tribunal.

These are the meaning of our Lord's words, and he applied these test principles to the Pharisees, and made them realize in their own hearts that they were blind to all that was really good and holy and true, and brought upon themselves a self-pronounced judgment that condemned their errors and their lives.

Let us see to it that in our clearer light, and fuller truth, we bring not upon ourselves the like condemnation.

CHAPTER XIII.

THE SABBATH ON WHICH JESUS HEALED THE WOMAN WHO HAD A SPIRIT OF INFIRMITY.

"And he was teaching in one of the synagogues on the sabbath: and, behold, there was a woman which had a spirit of infirmity eighteen years, and was bowed together, and could in no wise lift up *herself*. And when Jesus saw her, he called *her to him*, and said unto her, Woman, thou art loosed from thine infirmity. And he laid *his* hands on her: and immediately she was made straight, and glorified God. And the ruler of the synagogue answered with indignation because that Jesus had healed on the sabbath-day, and said unto the people, There are six days in which men ought to work: in them therefore come and be healed, and not on the sabbath-day. The Lord then answered him, and said, *Thou* hypocrite! doth not each one of you on the sabbath loose his ox or *his* ass from the stall, and lead *him* away to watering? And ought not this woman, being a daughter of Abraham, whom Satan hath bound, lo these eighteen years, be loosed from this bond on the sabbath-day? And when he had said these things, all his adversaries were ashamed: and all the people rejoiced for all the glorious things that were done by him." LUKE xiii. 10-17.

T. LUKE only records this Sabbath work of Jesus. He does not tell us in what city it was done, but only says, "In one of the Synagogues."

He was there teaching, for we do not doubt

that on every Sabbath day after his public entrance upon his ministry he preached to the people in a Synagogue or in the temple. His work-day, as he knew, was to be brief; hence he filled all its hours with the deeds which advanced the establishment of his kingdom. His language ever was, "I must work the works of Him that sent me while it is day; the night cometh, in which no man can work," and we know that he said, "My meat is to do the will of Him that sent me and to finish his work." He had ever before him a divine and definite plan. To its accomplishment he bent all the energy of his body and the purpose of his will. In doing this he never flagged in zeal or faltered in purpose. In the singleness of his eye to God's glory, in the fixedness of his will to do God's work, in the untiring industry which marked his labors, he sets us an example that we should follow, as near as we can, the steps of Him "who went about doing good." The eye of Jesus was as quick to see, as his heart was quick to feel for, the bodily afflictions of those around him. Seeing in this Synagogue "a woman which had a spirit of infirmity eighteen years, and was bowed together and could in no wise lift up herself, he called her to him." She does not seem to have gone to the Synagogue for the purpose of receiving healing, nor does she appear as one asking a favor of our Lord. Yet Jesus saw in her not only an object of merciful commiseration, but a case by and through which he could make known afresh, and with renewed force, the power which he held in his hand as Lord alike of the spirit world and of the Sabbath. At his call, this cripple, bent double, with face earthward, with body distorted, in whom hope of relief had died out long ago, and to whom perhaps life was a burden and a grief, came before the assembly, presenting to them all a mournful spectacle that should have excited their tenderest sympathy. As soon as she had reached Jesus he laid his hand on her and pronounced the healing words, "Woman, thou art loosed from thine infirmity." The words of our Lord are peculiar, different from those ordinarily used in his miracles of healing. They implied bonds, fetters, and these again implied a binder, a fetterer, one who had manacled her body with a chain, and bowed it together and kept it bent with a bond which no human power could break. Accordingly, our Lord says subsequently that she had been bound by Satan, that he was the slave-master who had thus chained together, as it were, the head and feet of his victim. Thus her infirmity is traced to Satan, whether directly, through some such permitted agency as was allowed to him in the case of Job, or the "thorn in the flesh" of Paul; or indirectly, to the resulting evil of some sin into which he tempted her, we cannot tell; all we know is that "Satan had bound" her, that she had been his bond-woman for eighteen years, that no power of man could loose this bond and make her body straight, and that she was thus in her own eyes and in the judgment of others a helpless, incurable, life-long cripple.

But no sooner does our Lord pronounce the words which by their potent influence dissolve the bonds than she lifts herself up, finds herself made straight, and at once glorifies God. The strong man, armed, had thus kept and deformed the palace of this body for nearly a score of years, but now a stronger than the prince of this world had come upon him, broken his bands asunder, taken from him his spoil, and let the captive go free, erect, rejoicing.

This act on the part of Jesus immediately ex-

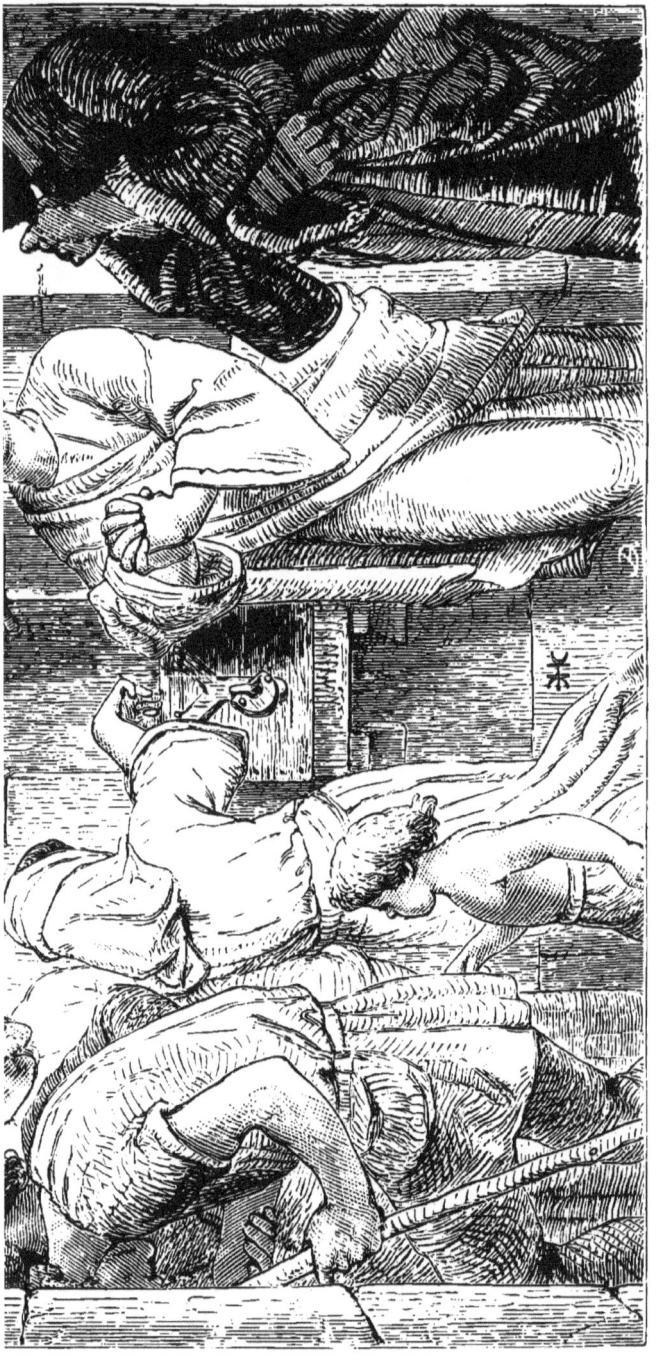

THE WIDOW'S MITE.

cites the indignation of the ruler of the Synagogue; and too much overawed by the miracle to say a word against Jesus, he turns upon the people and scolds them, as if they had done an act of wrong. Indeed, he rebukes them as Sabbath-breakers, saying, "There are six days in which men ought to work: in them therefore come and be healed, and not on the Sabbath day." He thus sought to do away the effect of the miracle by urging the charge of Sabbath breaking. He seeks to change the current of their thoughts, then doubtless flowing Christward in wonder and thankfulness for such display of divine power, into another channel, whereby the people would reproach both themselves and Jesus as violators of the fourth commandment. Through all this deceit and mock jealousy of the law of Moses our Lord saw, and replied, "Thou hypocrite!" causing the ruler of the Synagogue to feel that he had penetrated into the secret motives of his heart; and then he establishes the charge of hypocrisy by asking, "Doth not each one of you on the Sabbath loose his ox or his ass from the stall and lead him away to watering? And ought not this woman, being a daughter of Abraham, whom Satan hath bound, lo! these eighteen years, be loosed from this bond on the Sabbath day?" How pertinent and unanswerable was this illustration and question of Jesus!

If you can on the Sabbath loose the bonds that bind your beasts in order to give them water—bonds that have tied them to your stall, but a few hours, and beasts that have no souls—do you blame me for loosing a bond of eighteen years' duration, fastened on a daughter of Abraham, and restoring to her the free use of limb and body of which Satan had so long deprived her? Well might his adversaries "be ashamed." Their hypocritical cant about the Sabbath had been exposed, their own works upon their own cattle were made to testify to their hypocrisy. They were ashamed also at being thus exposed to the people, and subjected doubtless to the ridicule of those whose esteem and reverence they so sedulously courted. On the other hand, "all the people" (for we ever find that "the people" flocked to hear him, that "the common people heard him gladly") "rejoiced for all the glorious things that were done by him." Thus shame and joy were mingled in the congregation—shame on the part of the ruler and his friends, arising out of their conscious exposure and defeat, for truth always exposes and defeats error and hypocrisy, and joy on the part of the people, who recognize in these works of Jesus a pledge of love and grace which they eagerly sought, though as yet they understood not the full purport of his holy mission.

The time is coming when there will be a similar exposure of all the hypocrisies of men, when the gloss and glare of sin shall be rubbed off, when the masks it wears shall be removed, when it shall appear in its naked foulness and filthiness, and when all eyes shall see the miserable artifice and subterfuge which served to disguise guilt and make even sin itself wear the aspect and livery of goodness.

The time is coming when all Christ's "adversaries" shall "be ashamed"—ashamed at their folly in ever trusting to the lures of the "father of lies;" ashamed at their guilt in persistently rejecting so glorious and merciful a Saviour; ashamed of their personal sins, which will then lie naked and open before the eyes of the universe, when the secrets of all hearts shall be revealed. How will those who now reject

Jesus then "call on the rocks and the mountains, Fall on us and hide us from the face of Him that sitteth upon the throne, for the great day of his wrath is come, and we are not able to stand!" It is a hard position to occupy, that of an "adversary" of Christ. Yet all are adversaries who are not his professed and faithful friends. His words are, "He that is not with me is against me," and you can be with Christ only by a living faith that unites you to him even as the branch is united to the vine, and of all who are not thus "with Christ" he has declared, "Those mine enemies who would not that I should reign over them, bring them hither and slay them before me."

On the other hand, it will be a day of intense rejoicing when Jesus shall rule king of nations as he now does king of saints, when his word will be the world's law, his life the world's example, his truth the world's light, his salvation the world's hope, his kingdom the world's glory. Then how desirable will it be to be found among the "friends" of Jesus, to realize that the great Redeemer is our Elder Brother, one who has borne our nature, who has atoned for our sin, who has graven our names on the palms of his hands, and who has prepared for us the many mansions in the "Father's house" in heaven! In that "Father's house of many mansions" we doubt not that the ransomed souls will study over and over again "all the glorious things that were done by him." Not the few specimen instances recorded in the gospels, but those innumerable acts and words of love and mercy of which St. John says, "The which, if they should be written every one, I suppose that even the world itself could not contain the books that should be written."

The two parables which follow were evidently part of our Lord's teachings on the Sabbath; and though St. Matthew records both and St. Mark one (that of the mustard seed) in somewhat different connections, yet that constitutes no reason why they should not have formed part of his discourse on this day. For it seems that they naturally sprang up out of the bitter opposition of the Jews to Jesus, and are designed to show, first, by the parable of the mustard seed, that though the kingdom of God, as represented now by Jesus and his few followers, might seem small and insignificant even as a grain of mustard seed, yet by and by it would become a great tree, "greater than all herbs;" and second, by the parable of the leaven, that though the teaching of Jesus seemed to find but small lodgment in the hearts of the people now, yet, like a small piece of leaven, it would ere long leaven the whole lump and assimilate all to itself.

Our Lord introduces these parables with the questions, "Unto what is the kingdom of God like? and whereunto shall I liken it?" Not that he was at any loss to state what it was like, but for the purpose of eliciting their attention and to awaken thought in their minds as to the nature of that kingdom. Not waiting for an answer, he delivers the two brief but most significant parables to which we have already alluded.

Without going into any formal exposition of them, let us note a few of their more salient points. The mustard seed is, indeed, "the least of all seeds that are down in the earth" which produce ligneous stems and branches, and it was in this sense, doubtless, that our Lord spoke of it, alluding rather to the relative difference between the seed and the full-grown plant than to the seed in the abstract, because the seeds of poppy and rue are smaller still, though the plants never rise above humble herbs, whereas the mustard seed "becometh a great tree and shooteth out great branches, so that the birds of the air came and lodged in the branches thereof." This, of course, refers to its growth in warm climates, of which we have authentic accounts; thus a traveler in South America says: "The mustard plant thrives so mightily in Chili that it is as big as a man's arm and so high and thick that it looks like a tree, and the birds build their nests in them, as the gospel mentions." The exceedingly small, and to human aspect insignificant, beginning of the kingdom of God, is thus strongly brought out when it is compared to a mustard seed. And looking at it with merely human eyes, what could be more small and insignificant than this first seed of the kingdom of God in its earthly manifestation? The idea, humanly speaking, was absurd, that less than a dozen illiterate Galileans, the disciples of a crucified Jew, could overthrow the old religions of the world and set up a new one which should extend from the rising to the setting sun. They were to conquer the world to the sceptre of Jesus, and yet immediately after his death they shut themselves up in an upper room "for fear of the Jews." Great names, literary honors, the patronage of kings, the favor of the people, they did not possess. To mortal view it was the veriest absurdity to commission such men to convert the world, then just passing through its Augustan age, to the faith of the son of a carpenter whom the Jews had excommunicated, and the Romans nailed to the accursed tree.

Yet see how soon this small seed became a great tree! Fifty days after the ascension of Jesus three thousand were converted under the preaching of Peter. In less than three years churches were gathered throughout all Judea, Galilee and Samaria, and in thirty years Christianity had spread over Asia Minor and Greece, southward to Egypt and westward to Rome. In a hundred years Justin Martyr declared in an epistle to the emperor Adrian, "There is not a nation, either Greek or barbarian, or of any other name, even of those who wander in tribes and live in tents, among whom prayers are not offered to God the Father in the name of the crucified Jesus." In the fourth century the golden-mouthed John of Antioch (Chrysostom) wrote, "The apostles of Christ were twelve, and they gained the whole earth. If you go to India, to Scythia, to the uttermost part of the world, you will everywhere find the doctrine of Christ enlightening the souls of men."

Eighteen hundred years have passed away, and how stands the religion of Jesus now? Take a map of the world, mark on it the countries most celebrated for law, order, morality, domestic virtue, refinement, intellectual culture, free government, and there you will find that the religion of Jesus prevails. Why is this? Why is all that is great and good and lofty and inspiring in law, government, literature, art, science and morality only found among the nations of Christendom, while all that is debasing in intellect, tyrannical in power, degrading in morals, whatever strips man of his glory, society of its safeguards, government of its paternal care, woman of her true position, is found where the religion of Jesus Christ does not prevail? Can we solve the problem of the extension of Christianity on the principles of human philosophy? Gibbon tried it in his five celebrated reasons, and failed. Is it solved by the maxims of political science? Machiavel and Montesquieu and Bacon and Guizot each assert that its wondrous development is an anomaly in the world. Can we match it by any parallel fact in any country, in any religion, by any founder of a new sect? The voice of universal history answers, No! It stands alone, the wonder of the nations, as the triumphal monument of Jesus on the plains of a fallen humanity. "Of the increase of his government there shall be no end." This religion of Jesus will advance steadily, surely, triumphantly, over all the barriers and obstacles of earth and hell and Satan, until it shall become the one only religion of every kingdom and tribe and nation on the globe.

The parable of the "leaven hid in three measures of meal" refers to this same spiritual kingdom, but under another aspect. The mustard seed represented its *outward growth* and enlargement in the eyes of men, the leaven its *inward working* in the individual heart, its assimilative, rather than its accretive, power— the internal penetrating and diffusing energy of its truth, rather than its external outspreading and greatness. It is the property of the grace of God, when it finds a lodgment in the heart, to change the heart into the character of that which is thus leavening it, just as it is the property of leaven hid in a measure of meal to change the character of the whole lump of dough in the midst of which it was placed. Like leaven, it works silently, imperceptibly, surely, transforming little by little the entire affections of the soul; and without imparting to it any new faculties or affections gives new force and direction to their outgoings and influence, so that the things in which the natural man once took delight now afford no joy; the emotions which he once cherished he now represses; the plans which once absorbed his energies are now laid aside; the passions which once raged in his heart are now tamed; while the things he formerly hated he now likes; what he once shunned he now rejoices in—prayer, praise, reading God's word, attendance on the means of grace, the cultivating of a meek and quiet spirit, the bridling of his tongue, the effort to grow in grace, are now sought for and cultivated with diligence and delight. "Old things have passed away; behold, all things have become new."

As the operation of the Holy Ghost is thus leaven-like in its workings in the individual heart, so it is also in its effects upon the mass of mankind. For the Church, which is the aggregate of individuals, the blessed company of all faithful people, is in its inner life sustained and developed by the indwelling of the Holy Spirit. This work is going on simultaneously in tens of thousands of hearts, effecting there those changes and bringing out those results which in their aggregation are to alter the face of the earth and make it "a dwelling-place of righteousness." And as the woman in the parable took and "*hid*" this leaven in the meal, so the leaven-like grace of the Holy Ghost is *hidden from the carnal eye;* for St. Paul tells us, "The natural man understandeth not the things of the spirit of God, for they are foolishness unto him, neither can he know them, because they are spiritually discerned." The working of this gospel leaven does not appear upon the surface of society—it is covered up from outward observation; but beneath the surface, at the centre of the mass, at the core of humanity, it is doing its assimilating and transforming work, changing into its own likeness and character that with which it is brought in contact, and so this process will go on "until the whole"—the whole elect of God—"is leavened."

These parables are prophecies as well as didactic lessons. They were true then, and they foretell what has come and what will yet come to pass. This shows the prophetic ken of Jesus as well as his self-confidence in the triumph and regenerating power of his religion. Out of these homely truths and illustrations—so homely that the delicate-fingered rhetoricians would hardly have touched them because of their extreme plainness and commonness—out of these homely incidents Jesus has shadowed forth the inner force and the outward growth of his kingdom. And though he stood in that Synagogue on that Sabbath day, hated by the rulers and Jews, having made but little progress in gaining disciples, having aroused the enmity of the learned, the wealthy and the governing classes; yet he knew, in his prescience, that though he appeared to men then as insignificant as a mustard seed, yet that the religion which he was establishing would eventually spread far and wide, and gather the nations beneath its branches; that the doctrine which he then taught, as disagreeable to them then as leaven, offensive to their natural taste, would yet, in its silent operation, change the great mass of humanity and make it sweet and wholesome with the sanctifying power of the Holy Ghost. Blessed be God that these things are so!

CHAPTER XIV.

DINING WITH ONE OF THE CHIEF PHARISEES ON THE SABBATH.

And it came to pass, as he went into the house of one of the chief Pharisees, to eat bread on the Sabbath day, that they watched him. And, behold, there was a certain man before him which had the dropsy. And Jesus answering spake unto the lawyers and Pharisees, saying, Is it lawful to heal on the Sabbath day? And they held their peace. And he took him, and healed him, and let him go; and answered them, saying, Which of you shall have an ass or an ox fallen into a pit, and will not straightway pull him out on the Sabbath day? And they could not answer him again to these things. And he put forth a parable to those which were bidden, when he marked how they chose out the chief rooms; saying unto them, When thou art bidden of any man to a wedding, sit not down in the highest room; lest a more honorable man than thou be bidden of him; and he that bade thee and him come and say to thee, Give this man place; and thou begin with shame to take the lowest room. But when thou art bidden, go and sit down in the lowest room; that when he that bade thee cometh, he may say unto thee, Friend, go up higher: then shalt thou have worship in the presence of them that sit at meat with thee. For whosoever exalteth himself shall be abased, and he that humbleth himself shall be exalted. Then said he also to him that bade him, When thou makest a dinner or a supper, call not thy friends, nor thy brethren, neither thy kinsmen, nor thy rich neighbors; lest they also bid thee again, and a recompense be made thee. But when thou makest a feast, call the poor, the maimed, the lame, the blind: and thou shalt be blessed; for they cannot recompense thee; for thou shalt be recompensed at the resurrection of the just. And when one of them that sat at meat with him heard these things, he said unto him, Blessed is he that shall eat bread in the kingdom of God. Then said he unto him, A certain man made a great supper, and bade many: and sent his servant at supper time to say to them that were bidden, Come; for all things are now ready. And they all with one consent began to make excuse. The first said unto him, I have bought a piece of ground, and I must needs go and see it: I pray thee have me excused. And another said, I have bought five yoke of oxen, and I go to prove them: I pray thee have me excused. And another said, I have married a wife, and therefore I cannot come. So that servant came, and showed his lord these things. Then the master of the house being angry said to his servant, Go out quickly into the streets and lanes of the city, and bring in hither the poor, and the maimed, and the halt, and the blind. And the servant said, Lord, it is done as thou hast commanded, and yet there is room. And the Lord said unto the servant, Go out into the highways and hedges, and compel them to come in, that my house may be filled. For I say unto you, That none of those men which were bidden shall taste of my supper." ST. LUKE xiv. 1–24.

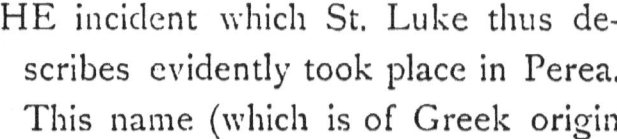HE incident which St. Luke thus describes evidently took place in Perea. This name (which is of Greek origin and signifies "beyond") was given to that portion of the country lying east of the Jordan, and including the Old Testament districts of Bashan and Gilead; the former, celebrated for its cattle, so often alluded to by the psalmist; the latter, for its medicinal gums and spices, which were exported by caravans to all the surrounding nations, and even as far south as Egypt.

It is exceedingly difficult and dangerous to visit that country now. It is wild and desolate, the home of marauding Bedouins, and shadowed here and there by the black encampments of these nomads, and uninviting, save to the antiquarian, who seeks amid its hills and plains and deserts, to explore the ruins of its once giant cities. It was in this region that Jephthah gathered his host wherewith to invade Ammon; that Ish-bosheth, the son of Saul, was taken by Abner after his father's death on Gilboa and made king of Gilead; that David, fleeing before his rebellious son Absalom, passed over Jordan by night and sought there a temporary shelter; and Elijah, "the grandest and most romantic character that Israel ever produced," lived amidst its wild people and wild scenery, and derived thence perhaps much of that rugged and uncouth aspect which made this man of God terrible to Ahab and Jezebel and the votaries of Baal.

At the time of our Lord the people were a mixed race, blending Jew and Gentile, that kind of half-breed border population which always fringes the edge of distinct nationalities and distinct religions as they touch each other.

As part of the lost sheep of the house of Israel he must needs visit these also, and hence he made a circuit "through all that region round about."

Accepting on one Sabbath day the invitation of one of the chief Pharisees "to eat bread" with him, he went to the Pharisee's house and sat down to meat. It shows our Lord's appreciation of courteous hospitality, and his readiness to mingle with all classes, and his fearlessness in the presence of even his most pronounced enemies, as the Pharisees surely were, that he should promptly accept the invitation thus tendered to him. We find him accepting hospitalities from various classes—the publicans, the peasants, the citizens, the Pharisees, the rich and the poor, restraining himself to no conventional limits or national prejudices.

It seems that the rich men in our Lord's time, acting on the glosses and teachings of the scribes, made Sabbath feasts not only for personal enjoyment, but for sacred hospitality. Special directions were given by the rabbins for the preparation of the Sabbath table: "Let a man arrange his table and spread the couches, and order all the affairs of his house, that he may find it ready and ordered when he returns from the Synagogue, for Rabbi Joses says that two angels accompany a man on the Sabbath evening on his return from the Synagogue, the one good, the other evil. When he comes to his house, if the Sabbath lamps be found lighted and the table prepared and the couch spread, the good angel says, God grant that it may be on the next Sabbath; and the evil angel must say Amen in spite of himself. But if this be not the case, then the evil angel says, God grant that it may be so (*i. e.*, no feast and no preparation for it) the next Sabbath, and then the good spirit must say Amen in spite of himself." The Sabbath feast was cheerful, but religious. A priest or scribe was usually invited to ask a blessing and guide the conversation, and so we find Jesus bidden as a guest to the tables of the rich, with the design, it may be, of securing a blessing from his presence, for the people generally recognized in him a great prophet and a good man.

During this meal Jesus sees "before him," not probably one of the guests, but one who had perhaps been aided in getting there by his friends, "a certain man which had the dropsy." Addressing the lawyers and Pharisees who were at the table with him, he asks the question, "Is it lawful to heal on the Sabbath day?" This question was one to which different Rabbis had given different answers, and was considered therefore as still unsettled. The question was propounded, not perhaps so much for the purpose of getting an answer from them, as to call their attention to what he was about to do, and to bring the act into the closest relation with the Sabbath day. It was a premonition to them that he was going to do one of his mighty works, and demanding their attention. To the question of Jesus no one replied. If they had answered "No," it is not lawful, they knew doubtless that Jesus would answer them to their own confusion. If they said "Yes," it was lawful, then they would put themselves in opposition to many of the received traditions of the scribes, and thus bring upon themselves their reproach and displeasure, so "they held their peace," watching doubtless with intense interest what he would do.

What he did, takes only one line to relate, but oh how much does it convey! "He took him and healed him and let him go." The long-suffering patient, burdened with a distressing and most uncomfortable disease, was at once relieved. The long process of absorption which takes place under the best medical treatment was here accomplished in a moment. The man who had come into Jesus' presence swollen, panting, heavy, hopeless of cure, went from that presence erect, with natural form, perfectly restored to health and strength. What a change! Beyond physicians' skill! beyond the healing virtue of anything in the materia medica of nature! Only divine power could disperse the tumid waters and restore the diseased functions to their wonted action. It was another of the many unsolicited works of mercy which Jesus wrought on the Sabbath day.

So soon as he had made this cure and let the man go—a cure wrought under their full inspection as to all its circumstances—he resumed his conversation with those who sat at meat with him and asked another question, in asking which he placed his whole justification in one pointed interrogatory: "Which of you shall have an ass or an ox fallen into a pit, and will not straightway pull him out on the Sabbath day?" The immediate reply in their minds, though it rose not to their lips, was doubtless, We would in such a case pull him out on the Sabbath, and

"They could not," says St. Luke, "answer him again to these things." It is not to be supposed here that silence implied consent; on the contrary, the language shows that they would have answered if they had dared, and were only withheld by a consciousness that by so doing they would encounter defeat. The miracle had been wrought, the man had been let go, the scoffers and objectors were silenced by an apposite question which carried with it an unanswerable argument; and so, dismissing, as it were, the case, our Lord now turns to another subject.

He had observed how the several guests who had been invited to this feast chose out the chief rooms or places at the couches or tables set for them, marking their petty rivalries and jealousies as to precedence and rank, and in that spirit which sought to improve every occasion for the teaching of sound truth, "he put forth a parable unto them that were bidden, saying unto them, "When thou art bidden of any man to a wedding, sit not down in the highest room, lest a more honorable man than thou be bidden of him ; and he that bade thee and him come and say to thee, Give this man place, and thou begin with shame to take the lowest room. But when thou art bidden go and sit down in the lowest room, that when he that bade thee cometh, he may say unto thee, Friend, go up higher; then shalt thou have worship in the presence of them that sit at meat with thee. For whosoever exalteth himself shall be abased; and he that humbleth himself shall be exalted."

The term "parable" here, as applied to this discourse, does not mean that kind of utterance so common to our Lord, whereby by similitudes taken from natural things he instructed in things spiritual, for in this instance it was a simple direction how to proceed in an imaginary case which might any day become a real one, and for the purpose of illustrating the important principle, that man rises to greater height by humility than by self-advanced claims to honor and precedence. The parable borrows its force from the social usages of Eastern life. The "rooms," or places at the triclinium or table, were graded according to the nicest distinctions of rank and worth, and the most scrupulous regard to etiquette was observed, especially on wedding occasions, to which Jesus here referred.

Instead of choosing for themselves what places they should occupy at the table, and thus distinguishing between themselves and others, they should feel that, as all had the same invitation to the same feast, so they should all take at first a common level, and let the places of honor be assigned by the lord of the house, who, having all the guests under his eye, and knowing their respective places in the social scale, would be better able to say to one, "Give this man a place," or to another, "Friend, come up higher." Thus self-judgment, self-assumption, were condemned. The pride of rank that creates so many heart-burnings, especially when self-asserted in public places and in an offensive way, is here rebuked, and justly so; for, what is so offensive as bloated pride puffing up its self-judged pretensions, and insisting on passing current among men, according to its own false estimate and self-esteem?

Having thus quietly yet effectively rebuked this unseemly contest for "the chief rooms" of the feast, Jesus then turns to the host and gives him a principle or rule by which to regulate his conduct on festive occasions: "When thou makest a dinner or a supper, call not thy friends, nor thy brethren, neither thy kinsmen, nor thy rich neighbors; lest they also bid thee again, and a recompense be made thee. But when thou makest a feast, call the poor, the maimed, the halt, the blind; and thou shalt be blessed, for they cannot recompense thee, for thou shalt be recompensed at the resurrection of the just."

The design of our Lord by these directions, judging from the tenor of these words and of words of somewhat similar import used on other occasions, was not to condemn those social gatherings of friends and neighbors which are so common (for he was then himself a guest at one), nor was it to declare when dinners or suppers were given that only the poor and cripples were to be invited, but it was to show the paramount duty of practical kindness and sympathy with the children of want and affliction, over the lesser duty of entertaining friends at set feasts, to the complete exclusion from heart and home of the poor and suffering. By putting the first part of his direction in a negative form, it was doubtless intended to intensify the affirmed duty of care for the neglected classes—not that all such feasts were prohibited or sinful, but such feasts alone, with nothing for the relief of the poor, the maimed, the halt, the blind, were sinful. The Mosaic law made special provision for entertaining the fatherless, the widow, the stranger, the poor, at their social feasts, and our Lord enlarges and amplifies and places on a Christian basis, what was local and exceptional in the Levitical code.

To spread a feast for those who will invite you in return is only to aggrandize yourself, and to seek the honor which cometh of men. To make a feast and call to it those whose poverty will not permit them to make any return in kind, is to be like God himself, who sendeth his blessings upon the unthankful and unholy—those who will not return him praise—as well as upon those who recognize his favor and thank him for his grace. Yet he tells us in a very marked way that, though the poor objects of our compassion can give us no recompense, we shall not go unrewarded, for "we shall be recompensed at the resurrection of the just." The deed will not be forgotten. He who provideth for the poor and needy wins thereby a blessing from God; and though he receive not any return in this life, yet come it will, when at the resurrection, all that they did for Christ's poor shall be adjudged as done for Christ himself, and so meet with a full recompense of reward. This was doubtless the scope and purport of our Lord's teaching.

The effect of these sentiments on one of those who sat at meat with Jesus was such that he broke forth into an exclamation: "Blessed is he that shall eat bread in the kingdom of God!" This interjection, from whatever motive it sprung, was seized upon by our Lord, who always found texts for his discourses in the words and scenes which daily met his ear and eye, to set before the guests the nature of the kingdom of heaven and the conduct of men in reference to their invitation to its blessings. This parable, suggested by the then surrounding circumstances of our Lord, and fitting in most strikingly with the time, the place and the words already spoken by him, is to be distinguished from the parable of "the marriage of the king's son" recorded in the twenty-second chapter of Matthew, though there are several striking similarities between them.

The parable of the royal marriage was spoken at a later period of our Lord's ministry, under circumstances different from those in which he was now placed, and is, in all its aspects, severer in its condemnation and results upon those who refuse the invitation of the great King.

The parable of "The Great Supper" sets forth the rich spiritual provisions which God has provided for his people under the figure of a banquet of fat things, the various calls sent by his older and later servants, the manner in which these invitations were received by those invited, the subsequent calling of others to supply the deficiency of the self-excused guests, and the final exclusion of those who were invited, but declined.

In Oriental countries, on occasions of great feasts, whether nuptial or social, the first invitation or notice that it will be given, is sent out long in advance of the time, to give to those invited opportunity to prepare themselves for the occasion. When the feast is prepared, then a second call is made by servants in the words of the parable: "Come, for all things are now ready," or as it says in the parable of the marriage of the king's son, "Behold, I have prepared my dinner, my oxen and fatlings are killed, and all things are ready: come unto the marriage."

To the first announcement of the great supper there was no objection. The difficulties arose when "the fullness of time had come," and the second set of messengers were sent forth with the invitation, "Come, for all things are now ready." Then "they all with one consent began to make excuses." The excuses were trivial and unsatisfactory. What though one had "bought a piece of ground"? The ground was not movable or perishable, that he "must needs go and see it" now. It would lie in the same situation and have the same soil to-morrow that it had to-day, and it was not necessary, therefore, to excuse himself on this account. What though another had "bought five yoke of oxen"? He could test their strength and quality to-morrow as well as now, and there was no pressing reason, therefore, why he should neglect the supper to "go and prove them." What though another had "married a wife"? Was she not given to him to be his companion for life, and could he not spare a day to attend at the feast? and this excuse, therefore, like the former, was worthless and insulting. They were all irrational, in themselves considered, and they were insulting to the Giver of the "great supper," as treating lightly and with indifference his invitation and his feast. They showed that they preferred farms, and merchandise, and pleasure, to association with him in the festivities which he had been so long and so elaborately preparing.

When these paltry excuses were reported to the "Master of the house," no wonder it made him angry, for it was treating him with disdain; and turning to his servant, and changing at once the purpose and character of the feast, he tells him to "go out quickly into the streets and lanes of the city, and bring in hither the poor and the maimed and the halt and the blind." The servant obeyed. These last made no objection—they came readily and gladly; but so extensive had been the preparation for this supper that, notwithstanding so many had been thus extemporized as guests, there yet was room. The generous host, not willing that any portion should be wasted or unconsumed, directed the servant, who had already, it seems, thoroughly scoured the city, to go out into the highways and hedges, and "compel them to come in, that my house may be filled," while of the originally invited yet refusing guests he said not one of them "shall taste of my supper." Thus our Lord illustrated to his audience the treatment which the gospel feast received at their hands. When first announced, it was heard of with joy, but when in the nearer preparation for it, the call came which required of them the giving up of something in which their heart was interested, the temporary forsaking of wife and houses and lands, in order to attend the great "Master of the house," then their unwillingness and indifference came out into a positive refusal to obey the summons. So it is now. The excuses of the parable are daily repeated, and men still delude themselves with frivolous reasons for not accepting the invitations of the gospel, forgetting the while, that Christ sees through their self-cheating hypocrisy, and knows that at the bottom of the pretendedly courteous words, "I pray thee have me excused," lies a bitter hatred of the glorious Giver. Of the great majority of those to whom the gospel invitation comes may it be said that they either "make light of it" by neglect, or else begin to make excuse for non-acceptance. They are all alive to their temporal interests—to advance these they will toil and make sacrifices; but when the salvation of the soul is set before them, when they are exhorted to repent, and invited to the gospel feast, then they are so pressed down with the cares and business and riches and pleasures of this world, that they have no time for the higher and eternal interests of their immortal souls. It is a sad but true portraiture of the treatment men give to the messengers, the invitation, and the Giver, of the gospel feast.

We cannot fail to observe the singular unity of thought which pervades all this discourse of our Lord in the house of this Pharisee, and how admirably the scene and the occasion is made the web which is so beautifully filled in with illustration, exhortation and parable. All his talk has some relation to what is going on in his presence. There is nothing far-fetched. His ideas spring up from the roots of things at hand, and his words, therefore, so far from being forced upon the unwilling ears of his auditors, flow out with a naturalness and gracefulness inimitably beautiful. We are thus taught by the example of our Lord how to mingle our discourse with the salt of grace if we would have it savory and wholesome.

What a dignity invests our Lord as he thus

sits at the Pharisee's table, and without cringing to rank, without truckling to influential men, without lowering himself to the level of their carnal minds and without giving any just offence, he yet tells them great truths in plain language, with pertinent illustration and with the majesty of a teacher sent from God, speaking to them "as one that had authority and not as the scribes"! If to all our feasts Jesus were invited, and if his words were the chief words heard there, how would his name be as ointment poured forth, and the whole house where he was thus received, and his words thus honored, would be filled with the fragrance of the ointment. So will it be in all its ineffable fullness of joy at the marriage supper of the Lamb in the guest chamber of heaven.

25 *

CHAPTER XV.

THE SABBATH AT BETHANY.

"Now when Jesus was in Bethany, in the house of Simon the leper, there came unto him a woman having an alabaster box of very precious ointment, and poured it on his head, as he sat at meat. But when his disciples saw it, they had indignation, saying, To what purpose is this waste? For this ointment might have been sold for much, and given to the poor. When Jesus understood it, he said unto them, Why trouble ye the woman? for she hath wrought a good work upon me. For ye have the poor always with you; but me ye have not always. For in that she hath poured this ointment on my body, she did it for my burial. Verily I say unto you, Wheresoever this gospel shall be preached in the whole world, there shall also this, that this woman hath done, be told for a memorial of her. Then one of the twelve, called Judas Iscariot, went unto the chief priests, and said unto them, What will ye give me, and I will deliver him unto you? And they covenanted with him for thirty pieces of silver. And from that time he sought opportunity to betray him." ST. MATTHEW xxvi. 6-16.

"And being in Bethany, in the house of Simon the leper, as he sat at meat, there came a woman having an alabaster box of ointment of spikenard very precious; and she brake the box, and poured it on his head. And there were some that had indignation within themselves, and said, Why was this waste of the ointment made? For it might have been sold for more than three hundred pence, and have been given to the poor. And they murmured against her. And Jesus said, Let her alone; why trouble ye her? she hath wrought a good work on me. For ye have the poor with you always, and whensoever ye will ye may do them good: but me ye have not always. She hath done what she could: she is come aforehand to anoint my body to the burying. Verily I say unto you, Wheresoever this gospel shall be preached

throughout the whole world, this also that she hath done shall be spoken of for a memorial of her. And Judas Iscariot, one of the twelve, went unto the chief priests, to betray him unto them. And when they heard it, they were glad, and promised to give him money. And he sought how he might conveniently betray him." ST. MARK xiv. 3–11.

"Then Jesus six days before the passover came to Bethany, where Lazarus was which had been dead, whom he raised from the dead. There they made him a supper; and Martha served: but Lazarus was one of them that sat at the table with him. Then took Mary a pound of ointment of spikenard, very costly, and anointed the feet of Jesus, and wiped his feet with her hair: and the house was filled with the odor of the ointment. Then saith one of his disciples, Judas Iscariot, Simon's son, which should betray him, Why was not this ointment sold for three hundred pence, and given to the poor? This he said, not that he cared for the poor; but because he was a thief, and had the bag, and bare what was put therein. Then said Jesus, Let her alone: against the day of my burying hath she kept this. For the poor always ye have with you; but me ye have not always. Much people of the Jews therefore knew that he was there: and they came not for Jesus' sake only, but that they might see Lazarus also, whom he had raised from the dead. But the chief priests consulted that they might put Lazarus also to death; because that by reason of him many of the Jews went away, and believed on Jesus." ST. JOHN xii. 1–11.

E come now to our Lord's last Sabbath before his crucifixion. His earthly life is drawing to its end. In less than six days he will be lying dead in the tomb. It will not be uninteresting, therefore, to mark how he spent this Sabbath, and yet but little is told us concerning a day which to him must have been one of mingled joy and sorrow—joy, in that his work was so nearly "finished;" sorrow, in that he had yet to pass such scorching agony on his way to glory.

He was now in Bethany, a word which means "the house of dates or palms," named thus, probably, from the palm-dates which grew there. It is situated on the eastern slope of the Mount of Olives, about three miles distant from Jerusalem, and not far from the road that leads to Jericho. It was unknown in Old Testament history, and comes into view principally as the home of Lazarus and his sisters Mary and Martha. Whatever may have been the beauty of this mountain hamlet in the palmy days of Israel, when the land teemed with inhabitants and its well-cultivated soil richly repaid the labor of the husbandman, it is now an unsightly place, with a few wretchedly-built stone houses, and the support of the miserable inhabitants who kennel there, rather than keep house there, is largely derived from the exactions made upon credulous travelers, in conducting them to the legendary house of Simon the leper, and to the so-called tomb of Lazarus. All that we gather in reference to the family in Bethany, where Jesus spent the last days of his earthly life, leaves the impression of a home of comfort, peace and love; and in the quiet of this domestic circle he found, doubtless, that repose which seemed so needful to him, amidst the intense labors of Passover week, wherein mind and body were taxed in all their powers.

Simon the leper is generally regarded as the father of Lazarus and his two sisters. Whether he was dead, and the name of the father, as was then customary, still clung to the house; or whether, being a leper, he was then under the ban of the Levitical law, and an exile from his home, a dweller in some waste place void of human habitation, we know not.

So many fanciful conjectures have been made in reference to him and his children and circumstances, and that too by commentators who are generally cautious, that pretty romances might be woven out of their speculations, though we must remember that all which they say is gratuitous, and probably apocryphal.

The household at this visit consisted of Mary, Martha and their brother Lazarus. The characters of the sisters are brought out in some delicate touches of St. John's pencil, and in the records left us by the other Evangelists. Mary, who seems to have been the mistress of the house and dispensed its hospitalities, was of a gentle, loving, contemplative cast of mind.

Anxious to drink in the gracious words of life which fell from Jesus' lips, she sat at his feet, and chose, as our Lord himself told us, "that good part which shall not be taken from her." Martha was of a more active temperament, full of housewifely cares and bustling with all the energies of a hospitable nature: in the words of St. Luke, "she was cumbered about much serving," was impatient at the meditative character of her sister, and hence asked Jesus, with words of haste and censure, "Lord, dost thou not care that my sister hath left me to serve alone? Bid her therefore that she help me." To this querulous request, showing how completely worldly things had gained an ascendency over her—it being in her estimate more important to serve tables, than sit at Jesus' feet and listen to his words—Jesus, who read her through and through, replied, not by doing as she wanted him to do, send Mary to her help, and thus countenance her undue secularity, but he gently reproves her, saying, "Martha! Martha! thou art careful and troubled about many things, but one thing is needful"—viz., that "good part" which Mary had chosen, implying thereby that Martha had it not.

The same traits come out again in the manner in which the bereaved sisters receive Jesus after the death of the brother, Lazarus. Martha, "as soon as she heard that Jesus was coming, went to meet him; but Mary sat still in the house" until Martha brought her word, "The Master is come, and calleth for thee. As soon as she heard that she arose quickly and came unto him." When Martha went to Jesus, she refrained from tears, and after giving way to one burst of feeling in the exclamation, "Lord, if thou hadst been here my brother had not died," intimates to him to ask of God to bring him back to her; for it was not until after a brief conference on the subject of the resurrection, and Jesus' announcing himself as "the resurrection and the life," that she was able to say, "I believe that thou art the Christ." When Mary went at Christ's call, she at once fell down at Christ's feet; and, though she greeted him with the same hopeless and sad words as did Martha, "Lord, if thou hadst been here my brother had not died," yet she entered into no argument, displayed no doubt, but burst into tears, and thus drew sympathetic tears from the eyes of Jesus—"Jesus wept."

The Sabbath at Bethany, on which our minds are now bent, was one after Lazarus had been raised from the dead. We do not wonder at the love, devotion and service of the sisters to Jesus, after receiving not only such a boon in the restored life of a beloved brother, but such a sure indication and proof that he was, as Martha said, "the Christ, the Son of God that should come into the world." Gratitude and religion, personal affection and spiritual reverence, combined to make him welcome to their house, and love for their risen brother, and love for the Master who raised him from the dead, united to offer joint homage to Him who had so sublimely announced himself to Martha as "the Resurrection and the Life."

The supper, or dinner, was given on the Sabbath. Jesus' disciples were with him. Other guests were doubtless there, as this seems to have been a thanksgiving feast for the recovery of Lazarus from the grave. Lazarus is present, and sits and eats at the table. Martha is there, serving, as is her wont. Mary is there also, but not serving in the sense that Martha is, nor yet sitting at meat, as her brother did, but during the progress of the meal she comes in, bringing with her "an alabaster box containing a pound of spikenard ointment, very costly." Approaching the table at which Jesus reclined in such a manner as that his feet were projected toward the wall, and thus rendered easily accessible, she goes behind him, breaks the beautiful vase in which this most celebrated and most precious of all odoriferous ointments was contained, and pours it out upon his head and feet in such lavish profusion that all "the house was filled with the odor of the ointment." Not content with this loving tribute, she bends over his sacred feet and wipes them dry "with the hair of her head," as if to show by this unusual service her intense gratitude and devotion to her Lord and Master. She had sat at Jesus' feet as a learner; she now stood there as his loving servant. She had received from him "that better part," that heavenly portion, more costly and precious than any earthly gift; and now she seeks to show her sense of its worth by that costly offering of spikenard, and that servant-like act of anointing his head and feet, and that still more unusual wiping of his feet with her hair, which in the aggregate evinced the most intense self-consecration to his service.

Jesus quietly accepted this fragrant tribute of Mary's love. He knew what prompted it, its perfect purity and its full significance, and we may imagine that he did not fail to express his emotions in language befitting the occasion. In the account of this transaction by St. Matthew and St. Mark, Mary's name is not mentioned. Perhaps she was living when they wrote, and it was not deemed best to attract attention to her at that time of persecution. St. John wrote at a much later date; and as she had then died, he made known her name, and told us what the other writers omitted, that she "anointed the feet of Jesus and wiped them with the hair of her head"—two incidents, each peculiarly expressive and, in their minuteness of detail, adding much to the interest of the narrative.

This act of Mary did not, however, escape condemnation, and even "indignation," on the part of some of the disciples, first "within themselves" in secret conference, then outspoken through the lips of Judas Iscariot, who, acting as the mouth-piece of the disaffected ones, asked, "Why was this waste of the ointment made? for it might have been sold for more than three hundred pence, and have been given to the poor;" and thus "they murmured against" the loving Mary.

As it is St. John only who mentions the name of the speaker, Judas Iscariot, and as he only tells us the hidden motive of his indignation—viz., "not that he cared for the poor, but because he was a thief and had the bag, and bare what was put therein"—we are led to infer that he first suggested the wastefulness of this anointing to the other disciples, who thoughtlessly chimed in with his ideas, led thereto by the unexampled value and profusion of spending a pound of spikenard on one person. As the common treasurer of the band of the disciples, receiving and expending what was put in and taken out of the bag or purse for their daily expenses, he had already proved himself a thief; and if the three hundred denarii, equivalent to about fifty dollars, which he says this ointment would have brought had it been sold, had been also placed in the bag, he would have had larger sums from which to peculate, and thus more readily gratify his lucre-loving heart. But Jesus rebuked the murmurers, saying, "Let her alone;" "why trouble ye the woman?" as if they were noisily reprimanding and faulting her for her conduct, and he then declares that her work was a "good" one and met his approval. "The poor," for whose relief you express such concern, "you always have with you, and whensoever ye will, ye may do good to them; but me," he touchingly adds, "ye have not always" —a distinct allusion to his speedy departure from them, the nearness of which no one but himself knew.

In this rebuke of Jesus to these penurious men, who were so indignant at what to them was wasted wealth, do we not find a virtual approval by him of every costly act which true love prompts us to bestow upon him? Is there not an intimation that nothing is too valuable to be expended on his person? and that genuine affection will ever lead to generous gifts for his use and service? And is there not the further intimation that, while the poor are ever to be objects of our compassion and charity, yet no wrong is done to them when, under the stress of some great mercy, temporal or spiritual, the heart, stirred to its depths with emotions of gratitude, seeks some outward and costly way whereby to show its devotion, and lavishes its wealth upon some work for Jesus in a manner which the envious and the unloving and the coldly calculating may denounce as unnecessary and wasteful?

We cannot now give personal gifts or personal service to Jesus Christ, as Mary and Martha did. But in the same spirit which prompted Mary to spend so large a sum in an alabaster box of ointment, which prompted Martha at the same feast to serve—viz., the spirit of grateful recognition of divine mercies—we can now commemorate God's loving-kindness to us by building a church, a parsonage, an asylum, an orphan house, by endowing a scholarship or a professorship in some school of the prophets as love's offering, making it our alabaster box of ointment to the risen and ascended Jesus.

Such gifts as these are often done, doubtless, out of a desire to perpetuate a family name, for mere ostentation, from a spirit of rivalry; but when done because Christ is loved, and the love seeks to express itself in some costly way, then will he approve the gift and accept the service and bless the giver. Nothing is too munificent for Christ if done out of real love for Christ: love consecrates it all to Jesus.

Having thus vindicated Mary from the indignation of these murmurers, Jesus proceeds to speak of the symbolical character of this act: "She hath done what she could;" "against the day of my burying hath she kept this;" "for in that she hath poured this ointment on my body, she did it for my burial."·

There is great solemnity and significance in these words. It was a noble commendation for him to say of her, "She hath done what she could;" no woman could have a higher eulogy, especially when spoken by Him who knows the thoughts and hearts of men and what she had done in his service. May not the words, "She hath done what she could," looking at this act of Mary from the point of view from which Jesus seemed then to contemplate it, mean that in his estimation, though undesignedly in hers, she, who would be unable to be near him when he died, had, almost in prevision of that burial, come now to do what she could do, anoint while living, the body which she could not see or anoint at his death? or had there been given to her that foresight, such as was occasionally given even to women at that day (as to the four daughters of Philip the Evangelist), by which she was able to discern the transaction of Calvary and the sepulchre, and conscious that she could not be with Jesus then, came now "beforehand to anoint him for his burial"? It was thus at least that our Lord accepted the unction and blessed her for it. Nor would he have spoken such unusually commendatory words had he not fully approved the act itself in all its apparent prodigality of expense, and in all the depth of its profound symbolism.

As an offset to his disciples' murmuring, Jesus gives praise, and their momentary indignation is set over against the declaration that the fame of that act would be coincident with the progress of the gospel, and ever redound to the honor of Mary of Bethany.

Consequent on this Sabbath scene in Bethany is Judas' visit to the chief priest for the purpose of negotiating the terms for his betrayal of Jesus. We do not know that he went immediately after being rebuked to them, though the language strongly implies it. St. John tells us that "*then* entered Satan into Judas surnamed Iscariot, being of the number of the twelve." That, doubtless, was the hour and place when, yielding to the temptation, "Satan entered into him." As if from that moment his body and soul had become Satan's by right of occupancy and willingly conceded possession. Satan entered that body as its master, and kept possession of it till Judas, under his instigation, "went and hanged himself."

We need not stop to speculate as to the various motives which prompted his immediate communing with the chief priests and captains of the temple guard how he might betray him unto them, for all is explained when we find him yielding up his whole being to Satan, and acting as his agent in this deed of crime. No doubt these enemies of our Lord were glad to find a betrayer, and chuckled with fiendish delight over the fact that one of his own household band—a professed disciple—voluntarily came forward to do what they so much desired—put him into their hands; for "the chief priests and Pharisees had given a commandment (or proclamation) that if any man knew where he were, he should show it, that they might take him." Little did they imagine that such good luck, as they would term it, would enable them to secure, and that too without any public tumult or rising of his friends, their victim.

"What will ye give me, and I will deliver him unto you?"

But indignant as Judas is, he wants to bargain with them and gain advantage to himself, and so he haggles with them for a price, saying, "What will ye give me, and I will deliver him unto you?" Here his covetousness, his money-loving heart, showed itself again with fearful significance. It was with that key that Satan unlocked Judas' heart, and went in and took possession of it, already prepared by its love of money for such a guest. Judas enters into covenant with the rulers to betray him to them "for thirty pieces of silver" (eighteen dollars!); he thus sells the Lord of glory at the then market-price of a slave, and in so doing unconsciously fulfilled the prophecy of Zechariah (xi. 12, 13), "So they weighed for my price thirty pieces of silver."

How little must he have valued Jesus, and how much must he have valued the thirty shekels, when he could barter the one for the other, and accept the latter as an equivalent for the former! We cannot pause here to discuss the many questions and points which arise out of this transaction. The character of Judas is still a mystery, and the fact that our Lord, with his acknowledged and often manifested omniscience, should select him to be one of the twelve, is also a great mystery. It is wonderful that he should have been for three years a chosen companion of our Lord, seeing him in public and in private, hearing him in the house and in the Synagogue, witnessing his miracles of power and of mercy, and yet be so base as to betray him to his enemies. Jesus may well term him "the son of perdition," one who is moved by the spirit of Abaddon (Rev. ix. 11), the king of the bottomless pit, leading others to destruction, and ending himself in perdition. This history furnishes many forcible lessons which it behooves all Christ's professing disciples to learn to their souls' health. How, for example, does his case tell us that outward intimacy with Christ, professing to be his follower, recognition by the world as one of his disciples, do not ensure salvation! How does it tell us also, that the most blessed privileges of communion with Jesus may yet be perverted to purposes of deadly crime, and, instead of softening, harden the heart! How does it tell us that the piqued pride or offended dignity will bide its time of vengeance in the hope of more surely compassing its end! How does it tell us the tempting power of money, and that the "love" of it is indeed "the root of all evil"! and how does it warn us with stentorian voice, " Let him that thinketh he standeth take heed lest he fall"! These are some of the many teachings of this traitor's life and doom. It is a beacon set up on the ledge of covetousness and disappointed ambition, whereon even an apostle was wrecked, warning off others from the treacherous rocks and heralding to all the future, the fearful fate of one nominally Christ's disciple, but really "a son of perdition." "Mark the striking contrast," says Dr. Schaff, " between the money-box of Judas and the alabaster box of Mary; his thirty pieces of silver and her three hundred pence; his love of money and her liberality; his hypocritical profession of concern for the poor and her noble deed for the Lord; his wretched end and her blessed memory throughout the Christian world to the end of time."

The character and act of Mary teach us lessons also of inestimable value. They show us how love overcomes natural diffidence in her anxiety to do something for Jesus. They show us that nothing is too costly so long as by it we anoint Jesus and make his name and his person "as ointment poured forth." They show us that Jesus appreciates and will reward such service and worship, while sordid parsimony or covetous longing, veiled under the pretence of care for the poor, will receive his just rebuke. And now this feast, "a life-feast over Lazarus," comes to an end. The guests disperse. The crowd which had gathered to Bethany to see Lazarus, the risen from the dead, as well as Christ, the Raiser of the dead, has melted away. The sacred hours are over, and Jesus has numbered his last Jewish Sabbath. His first recorded Sabbath was spent in Nazareth, the "city of branches," the last in Bethany, the "city of palms." His first Sabbath was marked by the murderous attempt of his fellow-townsmen to cast him headlong from the brow of the hill on which their city was built; his last was marked by that anointing which symbolized that diffusive fragrance of his grace which would eventually fill the world, when the name, and work, and glory, of Jesus should be known and loved, as the true Messiah, the anointed One of God.

CHAPTER XVI.

OUR LORD'S SABBATH IN THE SEPULCHRE.

"When the even was come, there came a rich man of Arimathea, named Joseph, who also himself was Jesus' disciple: he went to Pilate and begged the body of Jesus. Then Pilate commanded the body to be delivered. And when Joseph had taken the body, he wrapped it in a clean linen cloth, and laid it in his own new tomb, which he had hewn out in the rock: and he rolled a great stone to the door of the sepulchre, and departed. And there was Mary Magdalene, and the other Mary, sitting over against the sepulchre. Now the next day, that followed the day of the preparation, the chief priests and Pharisees came together unto Pilate, saying, Sir, we remember that that deceiver said, while he was yet alive, After three days I will rise again. Command therefore that the sepulchre be made sure until the third day, lest his disciples come by night, and steal him away, and say unto the people, He is risen from the dead: so the last error shall be worse than the first. Pilate said unto them, Ye have a watch: go your way, make it as sure as ye can. So they went, and made the sepulchre sure, sealing the stone, and setting a watch." MATTHEW xxvii. 57-66.

"And now when the even was come, because it was the preparation, that is, the day before the sabbath, Joseph of Arimathea, an honorable counselor, which also waited for the kingdom of God, came, and went in boldly unto Pilate, and craved the body of Jesus. And Pilate marveled if he were already dead: and calling unto him the centurion, he asked him whether he had been any while dead. And when he knew it of the centurion, he gave the body to Joseph. And he brought fine linen, and took him down, and wrapped him in the linen, and laid him in a sepulchre which was hewn out of a rock, and rolled a stone unto the door of the sepulchre. And Mary Magdalene and Mary the mother of Joses beheld where he was laid." MARK xv. 42-47.

"And, behold, there was a man named Joseph, a counselor; and he was a good man, and a just: the same had not consented to the counsel and deed of them: he was of Arimathea, a city of the Jews; who also himself waited for the kingdom of God. This man went unto Pilate, and begged the body of Jesus. And he took it down, and wrapped it in linen, and laid it in a sepulchre that was hewn in stone, wherein never man before was laid. And that day was the preparation, and the sabbath drew on. And the women also, which came with him from Galilee, followed after, and beheld the sepulchre, and how his body was laid. And they returned, and prepared spices and ointments; and rested the sabbath day according to the commandment." LUKE xxiii. 50–56.

"And after this Joseph of Arimathea, being a disciple of Jesus, but secretly for fear of the Jews, besought Pilate that he might take away the body of Jesus: and Pilate gave him leave. He came therefore, and took the body of Jesus. And there came also Nicodemus (which at the first came to Jesus by night), and brought a mixture of myrrh and aloes, about a hundred pounds weight. Then took they the body of Jesus, and wound it in linen clothes with the spices, as the manner of the Jews is to bury. Now in the place where he was crucified there was a garden; and in the garden a new sepulchre, wherein was never man yet laid. There laid they Jesus therefore because of the Jews' preparation day; for the sepulchre was nigh at hand." JOHN xix. 38–42.

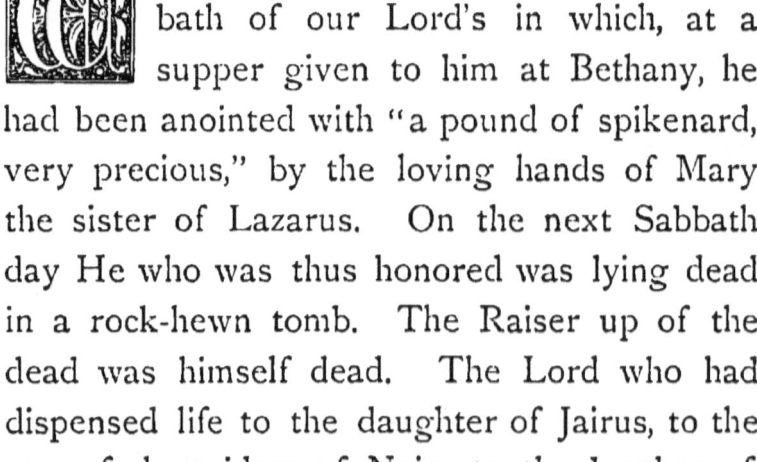E have just been contemplating a Sabbath of our Lord's in which, at a supper given to him at Bethany, he had been anointed with "a pound of spikenard, very precious," by the loving hands of Mary the sister of Lazarus. On the next Sabbath day He who was thus honored was lying dead in a rock-hewn tomb. The Raiser up of the dead was himself dead. The Lord who had dispensed life to the daughter of Jairus, to the son of the widow of Nain, to the brother of

Martha and Mary, was now himself lifeless, bound hand and foot with grave-clothes. We need not dwell on the crucifixion scene, nor on the taking down of Jesus' body from the cross, nor on the request of Joseph of Arimathea to Pilate to grant him the corpse that he might bury it in his own new sepulchre, for these things belong to the day of preparation rather than to the Sabbath.

Is it not something more than a coincidence that we find a Mary and a Joseph both connected with his birth and his death, presiding as it were at the Manger and at the Tomb?

"It may be noted," says Wordsworth, "that one *Joseph* was appointed by God to be the guardian of his body in the *virgin womb*, and another *Joseph* was the guardian of his body in the *virgin tomb*, and each Joseph is called a *just man* in holy Scripture." The garden of Joseph of Arimathea, that "honorable counselor who also waited for the kingdom of God," was near "the place where he was crucified," and "in the garden was a new sepulchre wherein was never man yet laid." As the bodies of malefactors after death were at the disposal of the governor, Joseph—one of the great council of the Sanhedrim, rich, good, just, and one who, being "a disciple of Jesus, but secretly," "had not consented to the counsel and deed of the" Sanhedrim—"went in boldly unto Pilate and craved the body of Jesus." Whatever may have been his "fear of the Jews" before Jesus' death, he had none now. He was willing to let the Roman governor know how he esteemed the crucified One, and was ready to give to the sacred body the repose of his own new tomb. Pilate, having first ascertained from the centurion that Jesus was dead, granted his request. Another ruler of the Jews, Nicodemus, "which at the first came to Jesus by night," also came to render such services as were in his power. He came with an offering of a hundred weight of spices (myrrh and aloes); and under the direction of these two honorable men, the body was removed from the cross, wrapped in "a clean fine linen cloth with the spices, as the manner of the Jews is to bury," and then they laid him reverently in Joseph's new tomb "hewn out in the rock, and rolled a great stone to the door of the sepulchre."

This transaction had been carefully watched by Mary Magdalene, and Mary the mother of

INSIDE OF THE SEPULCHRE.

Joses, and the women also which came with him from Galilee, as they "sat over against the sepulchre and beheld how the body was laid." So soon as Joseph of Arimathea and Nicodemus had departed, the women also returned to Jerusalem, and after preparing their spices and ointment for a more thorough embalming of the sacred body, "they rested the Sabbath day according to the commandment." Nothing could have been more simple and unostentatious than the burial of Jesus. As his birth, in all its earthly aspects, was one that was surrounded with no pomp or worldly display, so the burial was the hurried carrying of him from the cross to the tomb, without parade, without funeral wailing, without any pageant of woe. He was laid for his first earthly sleep in a borrowed manger; he was laid for his last earthly sleep in a borrowed tomb.

We cannot fail to note the contrast between the way in which the holy women who attended Christ's burial and the way in which the chief priests and the Pharisees kept that Sabbath. The Marys and the other women from Galilee rested according to the commandment. They would not even anoint the dead body of their

Lord on that holy day. We can imagine with what almost hopeless sorrow they spent its sacred hours—how in the privacy of their home they talked over the mournful scenes of Calvary, and spoke with awe of the wondrous signs in the sky and on the earth which had marked his crucifixion. We can imagine how they recalled one and another of his gracious words and his gracious acts, until their hearts glowed as they mused and spake. On the other hand, the chief priests and Pharisees, notwithstanding that it was the Sabbath, and notwithstanding that they rendered themselves ceremonially unclean by so doing, "came together unto Pilate, saying, Sir, we remember that that deceiver said, while he was yet alive, After three days I will rise again. Command therefore that the sepulchre be made sure until the third day, lest his disciples come by night and steal him away, and so the last error shall be worse than the first." Here was a confession that he was dead, as their language and purpose prove. Here was still seen their obduracy, for they style him "that deceiver." Here also was manifested a fear lest his prophecy might come true, and hence they would take all human means to prevent his rising again. Malignity, hate, craft, fear, fill their minds, and make them desecrate the Sabbath with unlawful deeds and words and emotions.

That Sabbath, we are told, "was an high day." It occurred in the midst of the Passover festival, and hence was celebrated with unusual solemnities and reverence. It was one of the three great festivals of the Jews at which "all the males were to appear before the Lord." It was kept in honor of the deliverance of the children of Israel from the destroying angel; when, in consequence of the sprinkling of the blood of the paschal lamb on the lintel and doorposts of their houses, he passed over the houses thus blood marked; and while "there was not an house in Egypt where there was not one dead," there was not a house in Goshen where there were any dead. Jerusalem on this "high day" was full of people who had come up to this holy festival. Many hundred thousand had gathered there to commemorate their national deliverance and fulfill the commands of Jehovah.

Yet how few were interested in the transactions of Golgotha, or comprehended the import of the wondrous scenes of that day—the darkened sun, the quaking earth, the rended veil of the temple! They furnished subjects of talk at the Sabbath feast, in the family circle, in the groups at the Synagogue, among the visitors in the courts of the temple, and then the festive hours rolled on as usual, and the Sabbath sun sunk to rest in the waters of the Mediterranean.

During the whole of this Sabbath our Lord lay in the tomb of Joseph; the sepulchre had been visited, however, by soldiers and officials; the latter, to affix seals to the stone that was rolled to the door of the tomb, so that it could not be opened without breaking them; and the former, to guard the place from any intrusion, and thus defeat the attempt, should such be made, to steal away his body and then say that it was raised from the dead. With these exceptions, we read of no one visiting the sepulchre on that Sabbath day. Malignant hate pursued him to the tomb, and planted sentinels at his grave to defeat his predicted resurrection, and keep the so-called impostor in his rock-hewn prison.

Such was the condition of things on that

Sabbath day. It was a period of suspense and awe in the moral universe. There was something sublime in the hush of expectation that filled the hearts of apostles and holy women and angels as the hours of that "high day" slowly rolled on, and the Roman guards paced up and down before the sealed and silent sepulchre.

He whom prophecy had foretold should rise from the dead; he who had predicted his own resurrection; he who had declared himself to be "the resurrection and the life;" he who had proved that he was such, by calling back to life the dead lying on the bed, on the bier, in the grave,—was himself dead and buried. He upon whose return to life hung all the issues of man's salvation was lying in his grave-clothes with his face bound about with a napkin. Earth and hell and heaven bent as it were over his tomb in mute expectancy, for that sepulchre wherein he lay as death's greatest victim, and the grave's proudest trophy, was the last stronghold of Satan, and that must be conquered before his atoning work would be completed.

There is something very solemn in considering Jesus, not only as dead, but buried—as lying for a time under the power of death, as making his grave in an earthly sepulchre. Yet as it was necessary that he should die—for thus only could he bear the penalty due to our sins—so also was it necessary that he should be buried. This was requisite, not only as giving additional proof of his death by increasing the number of witnesses to the fact—not only to fulfill the types of the Old Testament which foreshadowed this burial, as that of Isaac, bound for a time to the altar and then released by divine interposition; and Jonah, entombed for a season in the whale, to be rendered back to the land on the third day; not only to fulfill the prophecies which predicted that the Messiah should " make his grave with the wicked and with the rich in his death,"—but it was especially necessary that he should go down to the grave, so that *there, in death's own dominion*, he might conquer death and the grave and lead them captive at his chariot wheels. As it was only by taking upon him the form of a servant, and coming under all the outward conditions of humanity, that he was able as a man in human form to work out for us redemption from sin, so only by going down to the state and condition of the dead, and coming under all the conditions of deceased humanity, could he "destroy him who had the power of death" and break the bars of the grave.

The dead of the earth are to rise from their graves, and Christ, as the "first fruit," must be in a grave before he can rise, as the "wave-sheaf" of the buried generations of men. The final conflict of Christ with the powers of darkness was to be made by the buried Christ, and the tomb of Joseph was to be the scene of the struggle. In vain would have been the holy life and divine teachings of Jesus, in vain his many miracles and wondrous works, in vain the agony of Gethsemane, in vain even the blood of Calvary, *if, once in the grave, death could hold him there.* If, voluntarily coming under the power and dominion of death, he had been involuntarily detained there, it would have shown that there was a power there stronger than he to which he must submit. But death gets all its power from sin, sin all its activity from the prince of evil, so that if Jesus had been held in the grave against his will, it would have proved that he was not divine, was not the Messiah, and inferior in power even to a fallen angel. It was necessary, therefore, not only that Jesus should die on the cross, but that he should enter into the house of this strong-armed death and spoil him in his own domain, and bind him there as his conquered foe. It was the last fortress of sin, and it must be broken down before there could be the cry of triumph; for if Jesus had been held captive in the grave, all his followers would have been held there also, and no Easter morning, with its shout of gladness, would ever have risen upon that dark valley. And how striking is the thought, that as in the garden of Eden "the first man, Adam," lost, by the conquest of him by Satan, original innocence and perfect bliss and communion with God, so also in the garden of Joseph, "the second Adam, the Lord from heaven," by his conquest of Satan, gained back our lost inheritance, securing to us thereby an innocence purer than Adam's, a bliss more heavenly, and a union with the divine nature beyond anything that ever could have been in an unsinning and an unredeemed humanity. In the garden of Eden, Satan conquered, and "brought death into the world and all our woes." In the garden of Joseph, Jesus conquered Satan, and "brought life and immortality to light."

The two gardens have been the two greatest battle-grounds of the moral world. The fall and the recovery of our race date from these two points; and had not the garden of Joseph reversed the victory of the garden of Eden, the whole world would for ever lie in the region and shadow of death; the great stone which lay against the door of the world's sepulchre would never have been rolled away, and the whole race, in all its generations, as they went down to the grave, would have lain there with no hope of a resurrection to eternal life and eternal bliss.

And this brings before us another, and the only other, fact we shall now mention in connection with the scenes of this Sabbath day—viz., the comfort which it gives to the Christian that his dear Lord has himself lain in the tomb. As we look at the grave, in connection with our friends or in reference to ourselves, there is an instinctive shrinking back from its coldness, its darkness, its decay. It is so desolate to put the bodies of our dear ones into the deep vault and leave them there all alone—to go away and abandon them, as it were, to the dank earth and the crawling worm. It is painful to think that we ourselves must soon lie down in the dust and turn to corruption; that this body will be but a handful of ashes; that all its "beauty will be consumed out of its dwelling-place." We do not wonder, as we look at these things in the light of natural religion, that the ancients, and all who know not the gospel, should depict death as "the king of terrors" and the grave as a devouring monster. But, blessed be God! we do not feel thus, now that Jesus has been buried. By lying in the tomb he has, as our forerunner, gone before to show us the way—he has turned its darkness into light, its despair into hope, its gorgon horrors into brightest joys. He has shown us, by his occupancy of a grave, that we need not dread to lie where he lay. He has shown us, by his brief stay there, that we also are to rise to newness of life; and as he passed through the grave to his final glory, so will the grave be to us the gateway to our blissful immortality. The call of Jesus to each one of his disciples is, "Follow thou me;" and that following *will conduct us to the tomb* before it *conducts us to heaven.* Death may be bitter to the flesh, but it will only usher the Christian into "the joy of his Lord." The grave may be repulsive to the natural sensitiveness of the heart, but we only enter there to change our dress, for there we are to put off this body of flesh and corruption and put on the resurrection body, for Jesus " shall change our vile bodies, that they may be fashioned like unto his own glorious body, according to the mighty working whereby he is able to subdue all things unto himself."

When such joy is before us, who will complain that he must reach it by passing through the grave? Who would refuse to enter the palace of the king because the portal was low and dark and dismal, and he had to wait there a moment before he could be conducted into the throne-room, bright with imperial glory? and who will grieve that he must pass through the grave and gate of death before he can enter the palace of the great King eternal in the heavens? Our only thought should be to fit ourselves for the hour of death by having our life hid in Christ, for we can *die in* the Lord only as we *live in* the Lord; and unless we die *in the Lord*, there will be for us no rest, no hope, in the grave, and no resurrection to eternal bliss beyond. But the soul that trusts its all on Jesus, that rests satisfied on his finished work, that pleads nothing for itself but that Christ died for its sins and rose again for its justification,—such a soul cares not for what may intervene between this life and its joyful resurrection, but goes down into the dark valley undaunted, and crosses fearlessly the cold stream, singing as it goes, "Thanks be unto God who giveth us the victory through Jesus Christ our Lord."

With what touching simplicity does Bunyan, in the Pilgrim's Progress, speak of this when he describes the death of Mr. Standfast!

"When Mr. Standfast had thus set things in order, and the time being come for him to haste him away, he also went down to the river. Now, there was a great calm at that time in the river; wherefore Mr. Standfast, when he was about halfway in, stood a while and talked with his companions that had waited upon him thither. And he said, The river has been a terror to many; yea, the thoughts of it have also frightened me; but now methinks I stand easy; my foot is fixed upon that on which the feet of the priests that bare the ark of the covenant stood while Israel went over Jordan. The waters indeed are to the palate bitter, and to the stomach cold, yet the thoughts of what I am going to, and of the conduct that waits for me on the other side, doth lie as a glowing coal at my heart. I see myself now at the end of my journey; my toilsome days are ended. I am going to see that head that was crowned with thorns, and that face that was spit upon, for me. I have formerly lived by hearsay and faith, but now I go where I shall live by sight, and shall be with Him in whose company I delight myself. I have loved to hear my Lord spoken of; and wherever I have seen the print of his shoe in the earth, there I have coveted to set my foot too. His name has been to me as a civet-box; yea, sweeter than all perfumes. His voice to me has been most sweet, and his countenance I have more desired than they that have most desired the light of the sun. His words I did use to gather for my food, and for antidotes against my faintings. He has held me and hath kept me from mine iniquities; yea, my steps hath he strengthened in his way. Now while he was thus in discourse, his countenance changed, his strong man bowed under him, and after he had said, Take me, for I come unto thee, he ceased to be seen of them.

"But glorious it was to see how the open region was filled with horses and chariots, with trumpeters and pipers, with buglers and players upon stringed instruments, to welcome the pilgrims as they went up and followed one another in at the beautiful gate of the city. . . . And, lo! as they entered they were transfigured, and they had raiment put on them that shone like gold. Then I heard in my dream that all the bells in the city rang again for joy, and that it was said unto them, Enter ye into the joy of your Lord."

CHAPTER XVII.

THE FIRST LORD'S DAY.

I.—THE MORNING HOURS.

"In the end of the Sabbath, as it began to dawn toward the first day of the week, came Mary Magdalene and the other Mary to see the sepulchre. And, behold, there was a great earthquake: for the angel of the Lord descended from heaven, and came and rolled back the stone from the door, and sat upon it. His countenance was like lightning, and his raiment white as snow: and for fear of him the keepers did shake, and became as dead men. And the angel answered and said unto the women, Fear not ye: for I know that ye seek Jesus, which was crucified. He is not here: for he is risen, as he said. Come, see the place where the Lord lay. And go quickly, and tell his disciples that he is risen from the dead; and, behold, he goeth before you into Galilee; there shall ye see him : lo, I have told you. And they departed quickly from the sepulchre with fear and great joy; and did run to bring his disciples word. And as they went to tell his disciples, behold, Jesus met them, saying, All hail. And they came and held him by the feet, and worshiped him. Then said Jesus unto them, Be not afraid: go tell my brethren that they go into Galilee, and there shall they see me." ST. MATTHEW xxviii. 1–10.

"And when the Sabbath was past, Mary Magdalene, and Mary the mother of James, and Salome, had bought sweet spices, that they might come and anoint him. And very early in the morning, the first day of the week, they came unto the sepulchre at the rising of the sun. And they said among themselves, who shall roll us away the stone from the door of the sepulchre? And when they looked, they saw that the stone was rolled away: for it was very great. And entering into the sepulchre, they saw a young man sitting on the right side, clothed in a long white garment; and they were affrighted. And he said unto them, Be not affrighted: ye seek Jesus of Nazareth, which was crucified: he is risen; he is not here: behold the place where they laid him. But go your way, tell his disciples and Peter that he goeth before you into Galilee; there shall ye see him, as he said unto you. And they went out quickly, and fled from the sepulchre; for they trembled and were amazed: neither said they anything to any man; for they were afraid. Now when Jesus was risen early the first day of the week, he appeared first to Mary Magdalene, out of whom he had cast seven devils. And she went and told them that had been with him, as they mourned and wept. And they, when they had heard that he was alive, and had been seen of her, believed not. After that he appeared in another form unto two of them, as they walked, and went into the country. And they went and told it unto the residue: neither believed they them. Afterward he appeared unto the eleven as they sat at meat, and upbraided them with their unbelief and hardness of heart, because they believed not them which had seen him after he was risen." ST. MARK xvi. 1–14.

"The first day of the week cometh Mary Magdalene early, when it was yet dark, unto the sepulchre, and seeth the stone taken away from the sepulchre. Then she runneth, and cometh to Simon Peter, and to the other disciple, whom Jesus loved, and saith unto them, They have taken away the Lord out of the sepulchre, and we know not where they have laid him. Peter therefore went forth, and that other disciple, and came to the sepulchre. So they ran both together: and the other disciple did outrun Peter, and came first to the sepulchre. And he stooping down, and looking in, saw the linen clothes lying; yet went he not in. Then cometh Simon Peter following him, and went into the sepulchre, and seeth the linen clothes lie, and the napkin, that was about his head, not lying with the linen clothes, but wrapped together in a place by itself. Then went in also that other disciple, which came first to the sepulchre, and he saw and believed. For as yet they knew not the scripture, that he must rise again from the dead. Then the disciples went away again unto their own home. But Mary stood without at the sepulchre weeping: and as she wept, she stooped down, and looked into the sepulchre, and seeth two angels in white sitting, the one at the head, and the other at the feet, where the body of Jesus had lain. And they say unto her, Woman, why weepest thou? She saith unto them, Because they have taken away my Lord, and I know not where they have laid him. And when she had thus said, she turned herself back, and saw Jesus standing, and knew not that it was Jesus. Jesus said unto her, Woman, why weepest thou? whom seekest

"They saw that the stone was rolled away."

thou? She supposing him to be the gardener, saith unto him, Sir, if thou have borne him hence, tell me where thou hast laid him, and I will take him away. Jesus said unto her, Mary. She turned herself, and saith unto him, Rabboni; which is to say, Master. Jesus saith unto her, Touch me not; for I am not yet ascended to my Father; but go to my brethren, and say unto them, I ascend unto my Father, and your Father; and to my God, and your God. Mary Magdalene came and told the disciples that she had seen the Lord, and that he had spoken these things unto her. Then the same day at evening, being the first day of the week, when the doors were shut where the disciples were assembled for fear of the Jews, came Jesus and stood in the midst, and said unto them, Peace be unto you. And when he had so said, he showed unto them his hands and his side. Then were the disciples glad, when they saw the Lord." ST. JOHN xx. 1-20.

THE Jewish Sabbath is passed. The holy women have scrupulously kept its sacred hours, patiently waiting until the morning light of the first day of the week would permit them to go to the sepulchre. "Very early," therefore, "as it began to dawn," three women, Mary Magdalene and Mary the mother of James and Joses, and Salome, "having bought sweet spices, that they might anoint the body of Jesus," went thither to do that work of grateful yet sorrowing love. As they walked on, they said among themselves, "Who shall roll us away the stone from the door of the sepulchre?" They had seen this "very great" stone rolled on Friday to the door of the tomb, and they knew, therefore, that their united strength would not suffice to remove it. They knew not, however, that the stone had been sealed with the seal of the Sanhedrim, nor that the tomb was guarded by a band of Roman soldiers. Had they known these things, they would not have ventured into the garden of Joseph. When they reached the spot, however, they found the stone rolled away; "for an angel of the Lord descended from heaven, and came and rolled back the stone from the door and sat upon it. His countenance was like lightning, and his raiment white as snow. And for fear of him the keepers did shake, and became as dead men." The stone being thus taken away, they were at once enabled to enter into the sepulchre, but when there, "they found not the body of Jesus." They saw, however, two angels in shining raiment, "sitting, the one at the head, and the other at the foot, where the body of Jesus had lain," who told them, "Be not affrighted: ye seek Jesus of Nazareth, which was crucified: he is risen; he is not here: behold the place where they laid him. Go quickly, and tell his disciples that he is risen from the dead; and, behold, he goeth before you into Galilee; there shall ye see him." Hurrying back to the eleven apostles, the women told them what they had seen and heard, and Peter and John ran to the sepulchre. John reached it first, and "stooping down and looking in, saw the linen clothes lying; yet went he not in. Then cometh Simon Peter following him, and went into the sepulchre, and seeth the linen clothes lie, and the napkin, that was about his head, not lying with the linen clothes, but wrapped together in a place by itself." After this evidence of the truth of what the women had told them, "the disciples went away again to their own house," wondering at that which was come to pass.

Mary Magdalene, who had gone back to the sepulchre, did not now return with them, but remained. Her mind was perturbed with grief, and she did not take in the full meaning of the transaction. She only seemed to realize that the body of Jesus was gone, and so she lingered there, weeping and stooping to look into the vacant sepulchre. The angels there gently asked, "Woman, why weepest thou?" She saith unto them, Because "they have taken away my Lord, and I know not where they have laid him." Turning back from the tomb, she saw a person whom she took to be Joseph's gardener; and when this supposed gardener asked her the same question that the angels had done, "Woman, why weepest thou?" she answered, "Sir, if thou hast borne him hence, tell me where thou hast laid him, and I will take him away." Jesus said unto her—for he it was to whom she was speaking—"Mary!" That one word, uttered in his well-known tone, disclosed to her who it was, and she at once—exclaiming "Rabboni!" *i. e.*, my Teacher—sought to embrace him, by casting herself at his feet; but he said unto her, "Touch me not," cling not to me, "for I have not yet ascended to my Father, but go to my brethren and say unto them, I ascend unto my Father and your Father, and to my God and your God." She then went back to Jerusalem "and told the disciples that she had seen the Lord, and that he had spoken these things unto her."

As soon as the Roman guard at the sepulchre had recovered from their fright, which for a time almost palsied body and mind, they "went into the city and showed unto the chief priests all the things that were done." A council was immediately called, the facts stated, and the necessity of checking their being known at once became apparent. They could not meet this new and strange emergency, and so they resorted to bribery and falsehood, and "gave large money to the soldiers, saying, Say ye, His disciples came by night and stole him away while we slept; and if this come to the governor's ears we will persuade him and secure you. So they took the money and did as they were taught."

This is a simple record of the events of the early morning of this first Lord's day. How many subjects of deepest interest do they set before us! Only a few, however, can be noticed. Never did men more thoroughly overreach themselves than did the chief priests and Pharisees, when they asked Pilate to give them a watch at the sepulchre to prevent "that deceiver," as they called him, from rising from the dead. For the very means by which they hoped to prevent the resurrection were made the occasion of more firmly establishing it, and we should have lost some of the most striking and irrefragable proofs of this miracle, had not this request been made by the Jews and been granted by Pilate. But for this Roman guard, and the sealed stone, and the bribery of the soldiers by the council to propagate a lie, the testimony to the resurrection would have been wholly from the friends of Jesus, and liable of course to the charge of partisan complicity and design. But now, Roman soldiers and Jewish enemies are made to bear unwilling witness to this event.

The guard mounted at the sepulchre was probably the usual detachment of sixteen soldiers, detailed from the castle of Antonio for this special purpose. It is well known that the military discipline of the Romans was severe and exacting. To desert a post, or sleep upon a watch, was punished with death. This, these soldiers well knew, and such was the anxiety of the scribes and Pharisees in this matter that they had doubtless received instructions to be specially vigilant at so important a crisis. How impossible, then, to regard as true the assertion of the chief priests that his disciples came by night and stole him away while the guard slept! for while the body was gone on the morning of that first day of the week, yet the linen clothes and the spices which had been wound around him were still there, and the napkin that was about his head was folded together or carefully arranged in a place by itself. Had the body been stolen, the thieves would, in their haste, have taken the body just as they found it, and secreted it just as it was; they would scarcely have had leisure to carefully unwrap it of its bandages, the myrrh and aloes in which would make them stick so closely to the flesh that only with great care and washing could they be removed; nor would they have deliberately folded up the napkin that bound his head and laid it in a place by itself. The interior of the sepulchre showed no signs of haste or theft; on the contrary, there were marks of deliberation and thoughtful care, and proved that the disciples did not come by night and steal him away.

As to the other assertion, that Jesus was taken *while the soldiers slept*, the thing is so preposterous as scarcely to deserve an answer. The answer to the statement is, if they all slept (a thing impossible in itself, considering the severe discipline of the Roman soldier and the extreme vigilance required for this service), how could they know that his disciples came and stole him away? Can a man testify as to what took place when he was asleep? Go to any court of justice, and offer there the testimony of sleeping men for what took place when they were confessedly asleep, would their statements be received? There is not a court on earth that would accept or believe such witnesses. Yet confessedly, the body of Jesus is gone, and this is their only explanation of the removal. Now, either the soldiers were asleep or they were not asleep. If they were asleep, as they were taught to say, then their testimony is worthless, because they could not know what transpired in their slumber. If they were not asleep, then a few timid disciples, who had all forsaken Jesus and fled two days before, could not have ventured to assail a band of well-armed soldiers, placed for the very purpose of guarding the tomb of Jesus from spoliation, and could not have stolen the body from their special guardianship. Thus did God cause the wrath of man to praise him, and the plottings of the enemies of Christ to become some of the strongest props to the doctrine of the resurrection.

That the great council of the Jews, the Sanhedrim, knew that the disciples not only did not come by night and steal him away, as they bribed the soldiers to say, but that they in their hearts believed that Christ had come to life again, is evident from the fact, that in less than two months after the resurrection Peter and John were arrested in the temple for preaching "Jesus and the resurrection," and after a night's imprisonment were arraigned before the high priests and the council as to the power and name by which they had wrought the miracle of healing on the lame man at the Beautiful Gate of the temple. They replied: "Be it known unto you all, and to all the people of Israel, that by the name of Jesus Christ of Nazareth, whom ye crucified, whom God raised from the dead, even by him does this man stand here before you whole." A few days after, Peter and the other apostles were again arrested by the authority of the Sanhedrim and put in the common prison. When brought before the council, the high priest asked them, "Did we not straightly command you that ye should not teach in this name? and behold ye have filled Jerusalem with your doctrine and intend to bring this man's blood upon us." To which the apostles replied: "The God of our fathers raised up Jesus whom ye slew and hanged on a tree. Him hath God exalted to be a Prince and a Saviour, and we are his witnesses of these things."

Now, on the theory that his disciples had stolen the body, would they have thus spoken to the council? or, speaking thus, would not the council at once charge it upon them now that they had them in their grasp, and prove them guilty of the theft? But not a word do we hear from any of the Sanhedrim of any such thing. They commanded them to be silent, they beat them, and were so cut to the heart by what they heard that they took counsel to slay them, but not a word is lisped about their stealing the body, though the apostles on each occasion challenged them to the issue, by declaring that God had raised up Jesus from the dead, and that they were witnesses of the fact. Had the council believed their own story, now was the time to verify it and prove the apostles false. But no; they knew that their own statement was false, and never even attempted to deny or refute the declaration of the apostles.

Then, again, behold the wonder-working power of God in the circumstances connected with the rolling away of the stone from the door of the sepulchre! Had our Lord rolled away the stone, it might have been said that he was not dead, but had only swooned away, and was in a state of asphyxia or trance, and that, reviving under the stimulus of the spices wherewith he was swathed, he had by the exercise of desperate strength removed the "very great stone" which guarded the mouth of his tomb.

But by the earthquake, which evidently was local, and by the descending angel with "his countenance like lightning" and his snow-white raiment, there were proofs conclusive of supernatural interference. Had there not been these prodigies and angelic interpositions, we should have been tempted to doubt the truth of the resurrection, as making it exceptional to all the other great feats of Jesus' life. If when he was conceived by a virgin, it was announced by an angel; if when he was born, a multitude of the heavenly host sung his advent hymn over the plains of Bethlehem and a new star shone in the east; if when he was baptized, the heavens opened and the Spirit like a dove lighted upon him; if after his temptation in the wilderness, angels ministered unto him; if at his transfiguration, his very garments and body shone with resplendent lustre and a voice from heaven said "This is my beloved Son, hear ye him;" if in his agony in Gethsemane, an angel appeared strengthening him; if at his death on the cross, the sun was darkened and the earth quaked and the rocks were rent,—surely it was but in harmony with all these miraculous interpositions, that his resurrection should be signalized by angelic visits, and be accompanied by portentous signs. Had there been none, the grand climax of Christ's work would have wanted those authenticating seals, which marked the other epochs of his life as marvelous and divine.

There is something suggestive, also, in the incident that the manifestations of the risen Saviour on the morning of the resurrection day were to women only. It was by a woman's disobedience, that sin was introduced into Paradise; it was to a woman, that the first prophecy was given—that on which the hopes of the world hung for thousands of years, "The Seed of the woman shall bruise the serpent's head;" it was to a woman, that the announcement of the conception of the Messiah was first made; it was to a woman, that Jesus declared the gracious truth, "I am the Resurrection and the Life;" and now to Mary Magdalene and two others the risen Christ first presents himself on the morning of this first Lord's day. He thus ever recognized the moral and social power of woman. He placed her in her true position as a wife, a mother, a daughter, a friend. No one has done so much to elevate and refine woman as Jesus Christ has. His teachings and his Spirit have lifted her up from the degradation into which sin and man, and even the so-called religions of the world, had depressed her. Christianity has reinvested her with her original dignity as she came forth from the hand of God in Eden—to be man's companion in body, mind and soul. Not to be the slave of his power, the creature of his lust, but the handmaid of the Lord in all the high and holy service of a loving heart, and the intelligent companion of man in all the domestic and social arrangements of the family organization. The homage paid to woman in civilized nations, the contrasts which mark her position in the scale of heathen and Christian people, the protection which human law and sound education and a healthful public opinion throw around her, are all due to the religion of

Jesus Christ and his own line of action and thought in reference to that long-humbled sex. This work of Christ in behalf of woman has been recognized by her in all the ways and offices by which holy love could express itself for a holy Saviour. The history of Christianity shows how its largest fields of triumph have been among women—how some of the grandest heroines of earth and some of the noblest in the army of martyrs have been women. When men have doubted, women have believed; when men have fled from Jesus, women have fled to him; when men have sold him for money, women have washed his feet with tears. She has truly won for herself the tribute of the poet:

> "Not she with traitorous kiss her Saviour stung,
> Not she denied him with unholy tongue:
> She, when apostles shrank, could dangers brave,
> Last at the cross and earliest at the grave."

CHAPTER XVIII.

THE FIRST LORD'S DAY.

II.—EVENING.

THE appearances of our Lord after his resurrection thus far related, took place early in the morning of the first day of the week. Several hours passed before he next presented himself. In the mean time the word had passed from one disciple to another, "The Lord is risen." "The angels have told us so." "The women have seen and worshiped him." As the news spread, the hearts of the apostles were stirred with unusual emotion. The believing few who still clung to Jesus, despite his crucifixion, were reassured in faith and hope. The despondency and almost despair which brooded over the followers of our Lord on Friday evening, as they learned that he was indeed dead and buried, gave way to the exciting expectation of soon seeing him again alive. The rebound of their minds from gloom and sadness to the assurance that he had risen from the dead was great, and produced intense surprise and joy.

How they must have eagerly talked together, questioning one with another how it had happened! How they must have thronged around the women as they returned from the sepulchre to learn the truth of what they had seen and heard! How the unbelieving Jews would shake their heads and deny the facts, and perhaps deride their words! When the soldiers returned and told to the council what they knew about the earthquake, the angels, the rolled away stone, the empty tomb, the chief priests and scribes hastily summoned the council, brought before them the still trembling and excited soldiers, saw at a glance that their well-laid plans had been all thwarted, and that they must resort to prompt measures to prevent the soldiers from telling the truth as to the scenes which had transpired at the tomb. Their consternation and rage at their baffled schemes, and their hopeless attempts to destroy Jesus, formed a marked contrast to the exulting gladness, and the palpitating hopes, and the exciting

suspense of his friends, as they waited and watched for new developments in the wondrous scenes then unfolding before them. Between the true narrative of the friends of Jesus, and the false stories of his enemies, the fact, that Jesus' body was not in the tomb, was soon noised abroad, and all Jerusalem listened with mingled incredulity and belief. The angel whom the women had seen at the sepulchre had specially charged them, "Go your way; tell his disciples and Peter that he goeth before you into Galilee: there shall ye see him." It was a touching act of divine favor that Peter, who had thrice denied our Lord, and that too with oaths and cursing, should have been singled out by name as one to whom the fact of Christ's resurrection should be immediately communicated. Our Lord, who knew that he had wept bitter tears of repentance, was thus tenderly anxious to assure him of forgiveness, and not let him give way, as he might otherwise have done, to despair. Accordingly, we find that the next appearance of Jesus, and the first to any of the apostles, was to Simon Peter, as is distinctly stated by St. Luke, who says that he "appeared unto Simon," and by St. Paul in his discourse on the resurrection, who says, "He was seen of Cephas (the Syriac form of Peter), then of the twelve" (1 Cor. xv. 5), implying that before Christ appeared to the apostles in a body, called here collectively by the term "the twelve," he did show himself to Simon Peter. This accords with the special message of the angel to Peter, and with our blessed Lord's conduct to him by the Sea of Galilee. How this tender treatment of this grievously sinning apostle, and his gracious words to Mary Magdalene, another grievous sinner, proved Jesus to be "the friend of sinners"—"that he came" "to seek and to save that which was lost"! and what assurance is thus given to the vilest and the most degraded, that he is ready to receive into his favor even the very "chief of sinners"!

This showing of himself to Peter, which is supposed to have taken place in the afternoon, was followed by his appearing "in another form unto two" of the disciples "as they walked and went into the country." The words, "another form," imply that he seemed to them not in the familiar aspect under which they usually knew him, but as a stranger. These two disciples were on their way to a village called Emmaus, seven or eight miles distant from Jerusalem, and they talked together of all these things which had happened. While thus communing, Jesus drew near, "but their eyes were holden, that they should not know him"—*i. e.*, the appearance of Jesus "in another form," as St. Mark records, put, as it were, a constraint on their eyes, so that they did not recognize him, and regarded him only as a stranger who had come up to Jerusalem to the Passover festival. Perceiving their sadness he said to them, "What manner of communications are these that ye have one to another as ye walk and are sad?" They replied, "Art thou only a stranger at Jerusalem, and hast not known the things which are come to pass there in these days?" thus showing that all Jerusalem was filled with the exciting topics, and they wondered that, even though but a stranger there, he had not heard of the wondrous events of the past three days. Asking them, for the purpose of drawing out their hearts still more upon the subject, "What things?" they told him the current story of the crucifixion and the resurrection. They spoke to him of their hopes and their fears—what the women at the sepulchre saw and said, and what some of their own number witnessed there. Then he said unto them, " O fools and slow of heart to believe all that the prophets have spoken!"—"fools" not in the offensive sense of the English word "fool," but as if he had said, " O men lacking spiritual understanding and discernment, and slow to receive into your mind the deep truths uttered by the prophets!" Then he adds—" Ought not Christ to have suffered these things and to enter into his glory?" Was it not in accordance with the very teachings of the prophets, that Messiah should thus suffer before his exaltation to glory?—and then, " beginning at Moses and all the prophets, he expounded unto them in all the scriptures the things concerning himself." Instinctively there bursts from our lips the exclamation, " Oh that we had been there, to hear 'the Messiah' explain the Messianic prophecies! and the prophet 'greater than Moses' expound Moses! and the one to whom 'all Scripture' testified, open to them their whole meaning concerning himself!"

What a teacher! What teaching! The risen Jesus explaining the necessity of his own death and resurrection! No wonder that they said afterward, "Did not our heart burn within us while he talked with us by the way, and while he opened to us the scriptures?" It was a rare and gracious privilege, and their glowing hearts, heated with intense affection, warmed up their whole souls with wonder and joy.

Emmaus was soon reached—too soon for the ravished travelers, who sought to prolong the pleasing talk; and hence, when the stranger "made as though he would go farther," they constrained him, saying, "Abide with us; for it is toward evening, and the day is far spent." Having sufficiently tested their earnestness to enjoy still further communion with him, he yielded to their request, and sat down with them to their evening meal. It is a rule of the Jews that where three eat together a thanksgiving shall be pronounced by one. To Jesus, as the honored guest, was accorded this service, and in the performance of it "he took bread and blessed it, and brake and gave to them." Whether in the act of prayer, or in the manner of blessing the bread, or in the lifting up of his hands, whereby the prints of the nails were seen in their palms, or by some marked word or tone of voice, he made himself known, we cannot tell. Suffice it to say that "he was made known to them in the breaking of the bread." For then their eyes, which had been "holden" before, were now "opened"—they recognized Jesus, but, alas! he was gone; "he vanished out of their sight." Astounded by the whole scene, which had passed away like a glorious vision, the disciples, recalling the glow in their hearts at Jesus' discourse by the way, rise up "the same hour" and retrace their steps to Jerusalem. There was no abiding in Emmaus that night. What they had heard, what they had seen, must be told to the other disciples. There was no mistake now. The eyes of their bodies and the eyes of their minds were now fully open. They saw the Scripture in the light in which Jesus saw it; they had seen him also, and had walked with him, and sat with him and talked with him, and there was doubt no longer. The threescore furlongs that lay between Emmaus and Jerusalem were soon passed over—not, as an hour or two ago, in sadness and almost hopelessness, but with the quick step of earnest, glad-hearted men anxious to carry happy news to heavy hearts.

It was night when they got back. They found the apostles and disciples assembled together, but with closed doors, "for fear of the Jews." Knocking and telling who they were, they were soon admitted; but instead of seeing sorrow on the faces of the assembly, as they expected to do, the two disciples were greeted with the jubilant exclamation, "The Lord has risen indeed, and hath appeared unto Simon!" It was joy meeting joy, hope clasping hope; and as they told their own simple story of the walk to Emmaus, and how Jesus was known of them in the breaking of bread, we can imagine that the two currents of holy joy, meeting and commingling, would swell high the tide of holy gladness and make the room vocal with their ecstatic praise.

While thus engaged, "Jesus himself stood in the midst of them, and said, Peace be unto you!" The closed doors could not keep out the resurrection body of the divine Jesus, and so, unannounced, he stood suddenly before them with the blessing of peace upon his lips. Prepared as they in some measure were for this apparition by knowing that he was alive, they were yet unprepared for the manner of his entrance, and perhaps for his peculiar appearance. Hence they "were terrified and affrighted, and supposed that they had seen a spirit." He gently quieted their fears, and sought to reassure them by telling them not only, "It is I myself," but added, "Handle me and see, for a spirit hath not flesh and bones, as ye see me have." He then showed them his hands, his feet, his side, bearing the marks of the nails and the spear, as if to say, The same body that was nailed to the cross and pierced by the soldier is here before you. In describing the effect of this exhibition of himself to his disciples, St. Luke uses an expression which brings out with much emphasis the tumultuous emotions which then filled the hearts of his followers. His words are, "While they yet believed not for joy"—words which somewhat find their parallel in the homely phrase, "It is too good to be true," spoken of something earnestly desired, but yet hardly expected. The fact that our Lord had risen, and that he stood before them, was overpowering to all their emotional feelings; they could scarcely credit their senses.

The reaction of their minds from the almost despair in which they were in a few hours before nearly unbalanced their minds, and hence the shadows of incredulity still lingered, while yet a full belief had not gained the ascendant. It was just this state which our Lord upbraided them with—"their unbelief and hardness of heart, because they believed not them which had seen him after he was risen." To give still further evidence that it was he, he said to them, "Have ye here any meat? and they gave him a piece of a broiled fish and of an honeycomb. And he took it, and did eat before them." This act seemed to remove all doubt, and "then were the disciples glad when they saw the Lord."

Again does he enter into discourse with those present as to the "things written in the law of Moses and in the prophets and in the Psalms concerning him," thus conclusively showing the Messianic bearing of these portions of holy writ. Gladly do they listen as he "opened their understanding, that they might understand the Scriptures." The whole scheme of Christian doctrine seems to have been set before them, as he showed how "it behooved

Christ to suffer and to rise from the dead the third day," and that repentance and remission of sins should be preached in his name among all nations, "beginning at Jerusalem." He then, as it were, turns to his selected disciples, and says, "Ye are witnesses of these things," the chosen men to testify to the facts and truths I have now taught. He told them, however, that they were to remain in Jerusalem until they received "the promise of the Father"— viz., the baptism of the Holy Ghost—and thus be "endued with power from on high."

During this interview, also, as St. Mark informs us, Jesus gave them their great commission, premising it with the solemn benediction, "Peace be unto you! As my Father hath sent me, even so send I you." The terms of this commission were, "Go ye into all the world and preach the gospel to every creature. He that believeth and is baptized shall be saved; but he that believeth not shall be damned." The signs or credentials which were to attest their mission and certify to its authority were these. "In my name," says Jesus, "shall they cast out devils; they shall speak with new tongues; they shall take up serpents; and if they drink any deadly thing, it shall not hurt them; they shall lay hands on the sick, and they shall recover." Thus their commission was as broad as the world, as lasting as time, as authoritative as Christ's own mission from the Father. The evening wore on as these memorable words and scenes were spoken and done. At its close he called the eleven apostles close to him, and separating them from the rest, " He breathed on them" as a symbol of the divine Spirit which he was to bestow, and said, "Receive ye the Holy Ghost; whosesoever sins ye remit, they are remitted unto them; and whosesoever sins ye retain, they are retained."

By this mysterious act Christ prepared his apostles for "the promise of the Father," and made them receptive of the gift which fifty days after was to descend in Pentecostal fullness, amidst the sound of "a mighty rushing wind" and the "tongue like flames," indicative of the viewlessness, the resistlessness, and the illuminating character of the operations of the Holy Ghost.

With this act of Jesus, and with these words, by which he put into the hands of the apostles the keys of the kingdom of heaven, closed the first Lord's day on earth. Unlike the Jewish Sabbath, which began the evening before, this day did not begin until "early in the morning" when Christ rose from the dead. Unlike the Jewish Sabbath, which ended at sunset, this day did not end until after the evening interview of Christ with his disciples in the closed room in Jerusalem. Henceforth the Hebrew division of days gives place to the Roman, and the hours are to be numbered as in the Roman calendar.

We cannot close the narrative of the events of this first Lord's day without pausing a moment upon their significance and influence.

The transactions of this day are second in importance to those of no other day since the world began. The nativity of Jesus Christ was a great event, and was signalized by great wonders, the appearance of an angel of the Lord—a multitude of the heavenly host chanting glory to God in the highest, and the shining out of a new star in the east.

The death of Jesus Christ was a great event, and was signalized by great wonders—the mid-day darkness, the hiding sun, the rending of the temple veil, the quaking earth, the opening graves, the tokens of nature's mourning when the Lord of nature died on the cross.

If the birth and death of Jesus were thus accompanied by such miraculous portents, surely the day on which he rose from the dead ought, by analogy, to be alike signalized by signs and wonders. And so it was, "for there was a great earthquake," the angel of the Lord, with countenance like lightning and raiment like snow, rolled away the sealed and guarded stone; two angels remained in the tomb; and angel lips uttered the first strophe of that anthem, "The Lord is risen," which has been the Easter song of the Christian world for eighteen centuries.

The events of this day prove the divinity of Christ's words, works and person; for as the raising of his own dead body was a greater miracle than any he had performed in the flesh, hence, this being proved, all the others are proved thereby, inasmuch as the ability to do the greater includes the ability to do the lesser. It is said, indeed, that "God raised him from the dead" (Acts ii. 24, 32; iii. 15; Gal. i. 1), that he was "quickened (or made alive) by the Spirit" (the Holy Ghost). 1 Pet. iii. 18. But in the unity of will and act which exists in the Holy Trinity, actions and affections are ascribed at times to one and at times to another, according to the phase of truth which the sacred writers wish to present to our minds. And this is one of the leading lines of argument by which we prove the distinctive personality, yet divine unity, of the three persons of the ever adorable Trinity, Father, Son and Holy Ghost.

In saying, then, that the resurrection was the work of God the Father, the apostle means to remove it from its merely human aspect, and to assert it as being done in accordance with the will and purpose of almighty God, so that it should receive in the minds of the Jews the sanction and endorsement of Jehovah.

In saying that Christ "was put to death in the flesh, but quickened *by the spirit*," St. Peter doubtless meant to convey the idea that, as he was put to death by a carnal or fleshly power, he was raised up by a divine or spiritual power, of which spiritual power the Holy Ghost, "the Lord and Giver of life," is the divine embodiment and representative.

But when we look at Christ's own words, we shall see clearly that, though in the unity of the

Godhead, the resurrection was ascribed to God the Father, and God the Holy Ghost, yet the efficient and acting agent was God the Son.

"Destroy this temple," he said on one occasion (speaking of the temple of his body), and "in three days I will raise it up;" "I lay down my life that I may take it again." "No man taketh it from me, but I lay it down of myself; I have power to lay it down, and I have power to take it again."

On another occasion he said, "As the Father raiseth up the dead and quickeneth them, even so the Son quickeneth whom he will." His declaration to Martha was, "I am the resurrection and the life." "It remaineth, therefore," says Bishop Pearson, "that Christ, by that power which he had within himself, did take his life again, which he had laid down, did reunite his soul unto his body, from which he had separated it when he gave up the ghost, and so did quicken and revive himself.". Thus, then, by this crowning miracle, wrought in the tomb of Joseph, on this Lord's day morning, did Jesus stamp with the image and superscription of divinity all his previous words and works, and attested as true the glorious gospel of the Son of God. St,

Paul rests the whole superstructure of Christianity on the foundation of the resurrection, saying unqualifiedly, "If Christ be not raised, your faith is vain: ye are yet in your sins." Hence the efforts which have been so often made to overthrow the truth of the resurrection by the enemies of our holy religion. If that could be disproved, the whole superincumbent mass of the Christian Church would topple down, and the faith, and hope, and love, of the Christian world, would become one world-wide ruin, wrecking alike soul and body, for time and for eternity.

The events of this first Lord's day prove also that death and the grave are conquered foes.

If death and the grave had detained Jesus in the tomb, then would it have proved that he was a sinner like other men, and came under the conditions of our common humanity: "Dust thou art, and unto dust shalt thou return." But "his soul was not left in hell (the grave), neither did his flesh see corruption." He went down to the domain of death, that in death's own region he might "conquer him who had the power of death." He lay down in the grave that there he might wrest victory from the grave; and there indeed, single-handed, he encountered man's last enemy; and returning thence with the trophies of his triumph, "leading captivity captive," he puts into our mouths the shout, " Thanks be to God which giveth us the victory through our Lord Jesus Christ."

Do not these facts give to this day a holy pre-eminence and invest it with peculiar glory?

CHAPTER XIX.

THE CHANGE OF DAY FROM THE SEVENTH TO THE FIRST.

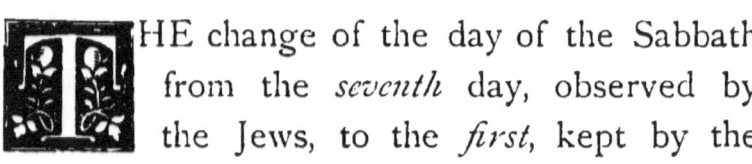HE change of the day of the Sabbath from the *seventh* day, observed by the Jews, to the *first*, kept by the Christians, does not affect the binding authority of the command, "Remember the Sabbath day to keep it holy," if it can be shown, that the change was made by competent authority, for sufficient reasons, and without destroying or infringing the two principles at the root of the command, viz., to give one-seventh of our time to God, and to keep this one-seventh portion holy to his name. A change has been made. The Christian world, with scarce an exception, keeps as sacred the first day of the week. And we ask, Was the change made by competent authority?

The only competent authority would be Christ

and his apostles: Christ as head over all things to the Church, which is his body; the apostles as commissioned by him to set in order the affairs of his kingdom on earth; and hence the Church of the living God is said to be "built upon the foundation of the apostles and prophets, Jesus Christ being the chief corner-stone." Whatever ordinances we find, then, established by Christ and his apostles, we hold to be binding on us, as being established directly or indirectly by competent authority. Now, we know that there was no express command to change the day from the seventh to the first, but the absence of an express command does not invalidate the change. For be it remembered here that the commandment does not read, Remember the *seventh* day, to keep it holy, but, Remember the *Sabbath* (the *rest*) day, to keep it holy. Hence, as the essence of the law lay in the setting apart *a holy rest*, which essence is still untouched, it was not necessary to make any formal legislation about a day which is, in its very nature, a variable thing, changing with the changing dispensations and shifting longitudes of earth.

God, by raising Christ from the dead on the

first day of the week, set HIS seal to the change of day.

Christ, by rising on that day, and by twice specially meeting with his disciples on that day, by imparting to them that day his "Peace," by breathing on them that day and saying, "Receive ye the Holy Ghost," and by giving to them that day their marvelous commission as heralds of the cross, set HIS seal to the change of day.

The Holy Ghost, by descending on that day in tongue-like flames, and with a rushing mighty wind, imparting to the apostles the promised power of the Spirit, giving to them the gift of tongues, converting three thousand souls, as the "wave-sheaf" of "the feast of first fruits" of the gospel dispensation, set HIS seal to the change of day.

The apostles, instructed by our Lord during the forty days which he was with them after his resurrection, when it is recorded that "he spake to them of the things pertaining to his kingdom," instituted the first day of the week as their day of meeting, established this day as the one on which to celebrate the Lord's Supper, ordered it as a day for the special setting apart of benevolent contributions, and so filled its hours with holy remembrances of Jesus and holy doings for Jesus, as to set *their* seal to the change of day.

The Church, acting upon apostolic precept and example, established its most solemn and permanent services on the first day of the week, and thus set *its* seal to the change of the day. While the Jews formed so large a part of the Church, it did not ignore altogether the seventh day, because the shock would have been too great to Jewish prejudices, but it gave pre-eminence to the first day, as we learn from Ignatius, Pliny, Justin Martyr, the Apostolic Constitutions, Tertullian, Dionysius of Corinth and other early writers. When, by the expansion of the Church among the Gentiles, the Jewish element and Jewish observances grew less and less, and when, after the lapse of three centuries, the Christian element had permeated and moulded the political world, the observance of "the first day" was enforced by the imperial edicts of Constantine, Theodosius, Valentinian and Honorius, and by the synodal decrees of the councils of Carthage, Illiberis, Sardica, Trullo and Laodicea.

There was, therefore, every reason why there should be a change of day from the Mosaic to the Christian dispensation, as the Bible leads us to believe that there was from the Patriarchal to the Mosaic. Nor was the change of day all that marked the introduction of the gospel. It has been well remarked "that the whole state of the Church of God underwent a revolution. Almost everything was changed in some way and to some extent. The Mediator was changed: Moses for Christ. The priesthood was changed: the Aaronic for the Apostolic. The law was changed: the Levitical for the Evangelical. The worship was changed: the gorgeous ritual and bloody sacrifices of the Temple, for the simple rites of the House of Prayer. The sacraments were changed: the Passover for the Lord's Supper, and Circumcision for Baptism. With all these changes, then, with everything thus made new, is it wonderful that the day of the Sabbath was also changed?" Would it not have been a marvel had it not been changed? When we remember how the Jewish Sabbath, like the Jewish worship, had become gradually encrusted with the traditions of the elders, so that it was perverted from its original intent of mercy, and void of its original end of holiness, do we not see the propriety of laying it and the temple both aside, that the new wine of the gospel might be poured, not into the old bottles, cracked and shriveled in the smoke of Jewish sacrifices and traditions, but into the new bottles of the Christian Church and the Christian Sabbath, untainted by superstition, uncorrupted by rabbinical glosses, and better fitted for the office designed of making the Christian rest day a Sabbath, a Lord's day for all nations, whom the Lord hath redeemed?

Had there been no change from the seventh to the first day, the Christian Church would have kept its weekly festival on the day when Christ lay buried in the tomb, that day of sadness and sorrow to the Lord's disciples—that day of dark forebodings and sepulchral associations, wherein we should have contemplated death's power over Christ rather than Christ's power over death; death's victim in his grave-clothes, rather than death's victor in his resurrection robes; and have passed over (or else kept two days holy) the day of days which commemorates Christ's rising from the tomb as the conqueror of death and hell.

And if to this weight of testimony and authority, which can neither be reasonably gainsayed nor resisted, we add the remarkable fact that the Church of Christ has kept this first day of the week as the Lord's day for over *eighteen hundred years;* that with this Church Christ has promised to be to the end of the world, and yet, so far from reproving or condemning the setting aside of the seventh day, and the introduction of the first as the Christian Sabbath, he has more specially blessed that day, has more peculiarly been present with his people on that day, has made it more than any other, the birthday of souls into spiritual life, and that these blessings have been vouchsafed, not only to the Church on this day, but to the persons, the families, the communities, the nations who have kept this day,—does it not give to the first day of the week the full sanction, as it has ever been marked with the full blessing, of God?

Can we need further evidence that the day was changed—changed by competent authority, changed for justifiable and appropriate circumstances, changed without infringing upon the letter or spirit of the Mosaic law, and yet so changed, that the two essential elements of the original Sabbath in Eden and the Sabbath of the Decalogue are strictly preserved—viz., the giving of one-seventh of our time to God and the keeping of this one-seventh time holy to the Lord?

This is the day, then, called "Sabbath," because the word means *rest*, termed in the Christian dispensation "the Lord's day," because especially consecrated by and devoted to Christ, of which God says, "Hallow the Sabbath day." To hallow a thing is to sanctify or make it holy, or to treat it as a holy thing and to use toward it reverence and devotion. It is in this latter way that we are to hallow God's name—a name holy in itself as expressive of the essence and attributes of a Holy God, but a name which we are ever to treat as hallowed, and toward which we are ever to conduct ourselves with reverence and devotion. But the Sabbath is a day that we can hallow or profane as we list, and hence, when we are called upon to hallow it, it is enjoined upon us to make it holy by hallowing it with public worship, with private devotion, with holy conduct and meditation, with abstinence from secular work and duties, and with an entire consecration of it to the Lord. The care with which God legislated for the Jewish Sabbath proves how jealous he was of its sacred character. In it they were to do no manner of work, "thou, nor thy son, nor thy daughter, thy man servant, nor thy maid servant, nor thy cattle, nor thy stranger that is within thy gates." No burdens were to be borne on that day. No fire was to be kindled on that day. In earing-time and in harvest they were to rest on that day. Buying and selling on that day were unlawful, and whosoever did any work therein was to be put to death; and a case of this sort is recorded in the Book of Numbers, where a man found gathering sticks on the Sabbath was by the express command of God stoned to death without the camp.

As if to give greater solemnity to this day, additional sacrifices were offered on it, and holy convocations, or assemblies for public worship, were to be holden, especially when the Sabbath was a high day, as at the feasts of Passover, Pentecost and Tabernacles. The Jewish rabbins had gradually so overlaid the law of the

Sabbath with glosses and traditions that our Saviour truly stigmatized them as "teaching for doctrine the commandments of men." Thus, according to the Jerusalem Gemara, " they must not blow the fire with a pair of bellows, because that was too much like the labor of smiths, but they might blow it through a hollow cane." They might make a fire and set on their pot, but they must not lay on their wood like the structure of a house—that is, too artificially. They might wash their feet, but not their whole body. Other rabbinical writers say that it is not lawful to roast an apple, nor to climb a tree lest they break a bough, nor to sing a lullaby to a crying babe. He who took corn from his field to the quantity of a fig was deemed guilty, and he who plucked up anything growing was regarded as reaping, and consequently guilty. These, with many other puerile and senseless additions, had been affixed to the observance of the Sabbath, by which, so far from hallowing it, they desecrated it, and made it a bondage and a grievance rather than a delight.

Our blessed Lord swept away many of these glosses, both by his word and his example, and restored the Sabbath to its legitimate end when he declared that "the Sabbath was made for man, not man for the Sabbath;" and he exercised his Lordship, not only by reclaiming it from Jewish traditions under which it lay smothered and distorted, but by showing us in his life how we should regard the day—with what works of love and mercy we should occupy its sacred hours. As he kept the Sabbath holy by meeting with the congregation for holy worship; by offices of holy benevolence and mercy; by seasons of holy meditation and devotion; by abstaining from all secular pursuits, and by honoring the day with the reverence which it claimed, so should we. Then, like the beloved disciple, shall we be in the Spirit on the Lord's day, and thus fulfill the command, Hallow the Sabbath day.

www.ingramcontent.com/pod-product-compliance
Lightning Source LLC
Chambersburg PA
CBHW022122290426
44112CB00008B/773